GOD IS OUR EVERYTHING!

THESE 10 CHAPTERS WITH SCRIPTURES WILL TELL
YOU HOW TO MAKE GOD YOUR EVERYTHING.

REVEREND DOCTOR OGDEN L. KING II

REVEREND DOCTOR OGDEN KING II

Been an ordain servant of God preaching the gospel for 20 plus years. He started at Believers For Christ Ministry, Walter Davis Sr. Pastor. Then he started evangelizing at various churches including New Life Church of God in Christ; the late, Nathaniel D. Carter, Pastor. He also had the privilege to work under the late, Honorable Chief Apostle Fred Jacob out of Alexandra, Louisiana. Later he became Assistant Pastor at Mt. Pleasant Baptist Church in Melville, Louisiana, Johnny Offord, Pastor. Now he resides at Liberty Christian Center where he was ordained Pastor by Apostle Dr. Elbert Bolden.

The path to ministry for Rev. King was blessed with ups and downs, hardship, triumphs, and illnesses that led him in a wheelchair twice where he had to learn how to walk talk and use his hands all over again. But with the power of God and his Grace and Mercy, God delivered him out of the wheelchair. That is just part of his testimony to show why God Is Our Everything! Music was always a dream of his. He is the youngest of 12, where his parents raised them up going to Church every weekend. At the age of 13, he began singing with a rhythm & blues (R&B) band called Merlin & The Super flies. At Opelousas Senior High School, Ogden played football, the track team and sang in the school choir. He graduated from high school and attended Delta Business College and Louisiana State University – Eunice. He joined the SYNBADD BAND and started learning to play the bass guitar where he had the chance to play with a gospel band at the age of 18. Finally, he got the chance to play semi-pro football with the Lafayette Angels and later a failed attempt at NFL professional football because of a back and knee injury.

However, after receiving injury the football career idea was over. Ogden then returned to his first love, Music. With relatives and close friends, the GRATITUDE BAND was formed. The band performed nationwide for a while then that led to the forming of G.K.G.L. SPIRIT Gospel Group. He really enjoyed serving the Lord in song and praise. For 18 years the group traveled, performed and recorded Gospel Music which I will tell more in the Biography that will be in the next book.

It was doing this time that he decided to become a Minister. Rev. King recalls, "After we came home off tour one day. Elbert Bolden (a Minister at that time) came and prophesied to Ogden King and band member Kip Guilbeau. Pastor Bolden said that we're going to be working for the Lord someday. At that time, we didn't take it to heart. Now, just a few years later here we are both working for the Lord.

In 2006 Liberty Christian Center was born. Pastor Elbert Bolden asked Rev. King to come on board as his Assistant Pastor. In 2012 Rev. King became Pastor of the Center, under the Leadership of Apostle Dr. Elbert Bolden. In addition, in 2012 Rev. King studied at Andersonville Theological Seminary College and earned his Doctors Degree in Biblical Studies from Sacramento Theological Seminary College. He had already received his Master's Degree in Biblical Studies (2004), Bachelor Degree (2002) and Associate of Church Ministry Degree (2000) from The Sure Foundation Theological Institute College.

Today the Reverend Doctor Ogden L. King II still preaching the gospel of Faith and Prayer. This is his second book and letting the world know that "God Is Our Everything!" One of his favorite scriptures on how to make God Our Everything. 2nd Chronicles chapter 7 verse 14; If my people, which are called by my name, shall humble themselves, and pray, and seek my face, and turn from their wicked ways; then will I hear from heaven, and will forgive their sin, and will heal their land.

With all the troubles in the land today we need to turn back to God. To do that we need to Humble ourselves, Pray, Seek God face and turn from our wicked ways. Then will He hear from heaven, and forgive our sin and heal this wicked land we are living in. "God wants to be our everything.

Love You and God Love You More!

ISBN: 978-1-963565-07-2 (Paperback)

Library of Congress Control Number: 2024907003

Printed in the United States of America

Published by

info@thequippyquill.com
(302) 295-2278

GOD IS OUR EVERYTHING

Chapter 1 Through 10

Contents

CHAPTER ONE
God is Our Strength

Amen let's give Jesus a hand praise! Glory Hallelujah let's give him praise. cause he's so worthy to be praised! Amen and bless God. First, I like to thank God for allowing us to be here on the Sabbath day the holiest day of the week, where our Lord has set aside and made a commandment the fourth, Commandment that we keep this day holy. Amen now I want everybody to Bow their head, close their eyes and to go to God in prayer. Oh, gracious Eternal Father, Father of Abraham Isaac and Jacob our father Yahweh Elohim The Great I Am the creator, of the heavens and the Earth Jehovah Jira our provider, father God we thank, you for being our provider Lord because, we know by Your Word Lord God we can, stand strong because your word is true, and just your word will do not go out and come back void father God, we ask you, this day to decrease us and increase you, let it be all of you and none of us Lord, allow us to take self and put self to the side. Lord, we ask you to use us, for your glory, Lord word our heart our minds and our lips Lord Almighty keep us in your perfect will and Lord as we stand, we thank you for watching, over us. We thank you Lord God for allowing nature to touch our eyes and wake us. Lord, we thank you for this brand-new day, with this brand-new mercy and brand-new Grace, Lord God. We thank you for keeping your hand upon our kids Lord upon us our neighborhood, city, Parish, State, Country and this wonderful world that you have given unto us. Lord, we ask you to use us for your glory Lord and we will be, careful to make sure that we give you, all the honor all the glory and all the praise. In Jesus most precious and holy name we pray amen and bless God. Now let's give Jesus another hand praise. Glory Hallelujah let's give him praise. cause he's so worthy to be praised amen and bless God.

Now I like to always ask God for message for you and I and why I always say I because we all came short of the glory of God, the only perfect one that walked this Earth was the Messiah, the savior of the whole entire world yes, his name is Jesus and without him where would

we, be? and God is so faithful to give us a message. now before I start my introduction, I like to always start off with a Question. Is the Lord our strength? Now most of us that have been, through trials and errors of our life know that God had brought us to it, and He brought us through it, Hallelujahs. That's one thing about this Mighty God that we serve, if you believe and trust in him, he will bring us out of any situation, that might seem impossible. He is very able to do it amen. So, the answer is yes, He is our strength, shield and Salvation Amen. I like to always ask, God for a blessing once again, for you and I cause we all need a blessing in these lateral days. Give him praise! We all need a blessing in these lateral days. And the blessing is may, God give us the power to trust in him, not man that's why the scripture say trust in the Lord with all thine heart and lean not, to your own understanding but in all thy ways acknowledge Him and He Shall direct, your path, let's give him praise, he's so worthy, we can't never give him enough praise amen and bless God. I like to always say in Jesus Christ holy name, amen. Oh, there go brother King again, with Jesus Christ Holy Name! Well, why in Jesus Christ Holy Name, well I'm glad you ask because in the gospel, writer John 1 verse 1 say in the beginning in the very beginning was the word yes sir and the Word was with God, now I like what the Messiah the savior of the whole entire world, Yashua better known as Jesus say I am in my father and my father in I and he told, the disciples when you have seen me you, have seen the father. Then the scripture says, and the Word was God that, means the word took on flesh let's stop, there for a second if the word is God? That means he cannot lie cause in the Book of Numbers chapter 23: 19 say God is, not a man to where he should lie nor the son of man, that He should repent, and verse 20 say he commanded a blessing, and he cannot reverse it. So that means, whatever his words say he can't, reverse it. God will not go against his word amen. And the Messiah the savior of the entire world the Word of God Jesus said anything, hear me well anything you ask in my name, it shall be given unto you by the Father which are in heaven let's give Jesus, a hand praise. What do you need today, My brothers and sisters? What do you need? Because God is able amen. Now that's enough introduction for
today amen.

So, now we are going to go to the word today is. God's strength is made perfect in our, weakness. Now we're going to go to our old Brother David in the Book of Psalms David the Book of Psalms chapter 73 verse 26 and we going to see, what our old Brother David had to talk about old David was from the Judah tribe Judah the son of Jacob. And it reads verse 26. Said, My Flesh that old flesh My Flesh and my heart fail it, but God is the strength of my heart amen. God is the strength of my heart and my portion forever. That means that God is our strength. Amen! You see our brother David was talking to us telling us that God is our strength amen.

Now let us go to Isaiah chapter 40. Isaiah the prophet Isaiah. He was the one. Prophesied about the Messiah coming, and he came. 40 verse 31 chapter. And it reads; But they that waited upon the Lord shall renew their strength. God is our strength you, will renew your strength through the words of God. They shall Mount up with wings as eagles, they shall run and not be weary and they shall walk and not faint, in other words if we believe and trust in the Lord, and be obedient to his words, God is, our strength amens.

Let us go to Isaiah chapter 41verse 10 Hallelujah, and I love what the Lord says he always tells us repeatedly fear not. So, that let us know, when we are serving a mighty God that created the Heaven and the Earth, we shouldn't worry about nothing amen. Because there's nothing too hard for the god that we serve amen and he tell us repeatedly fear not don't worry about it just trust in him amen so it says, fear thou not for I am with thee be not dismayed for I am thy God. That let us know that he is our God when we trust in him and be obedient to him amen, he said I will strengthen thee, God will give us strength. God is our strength. I will help thee, God will help thee he said yeah, I will uphold thee with thy right hand of my righteousness not man righteousness, but God's righteousness amens.

Let us go to Second Corinthians chapter 12 verse 9 And he said unto me, My grace is sufficient for thee: for my strength is made perfect in weakness, (God is our strength) and then it said; Most gladly therefore will I rather glory in my infirmities that the power of Christ may rest upon me. so that let us know God is our strength amen.

Now let's go back to old Brother David Hallelujah back to Psalms chapter 28 verse 7 through 8, I like our old boy David he was not perfect, but he was called a man after God's Own Heart he know how to praise God. That's the number one thing knowing, how to praise God giving God all the honor glory and praise you see we have a problem right their man always wants the glory every time they do something not, knowing that God is allowing them to do that. Man wants the glory. We must give God the praise, the glory and all the honor amen. It is all about God, that's right he is the one that, paid the price for us amen.

So that's Psalms 28 verse 7 through 8, and listen to what it says, The Lord is my strength, see David let it be known that. God is our strength and my shield my heart trust in Who him, and I am helped therefore my heart greatly rejoice; and with my song will I praise him. You see you got to give God all the praise because he is the one. Our life is already predestined, he made it possible. You know some people love to say I did, this, I did that, I made myself. Know God made it possible for you to do whatever, that there was that you achieved in life. And verse eight says, The Lord is the strength, and he is the saving strength of his anointing amen. God is our strength amen.

Now let's go to Psalm 31 verse 24. Be of good courage, and he shall strengthen, your heart, all ye that hope in the lord. (God is our strength). He is the one that strengthens us. Nobody else can do it. Man can't do it, but God can! Amen. He will give you the ability to go through anything that you might have to face in life, and he will be able to do it. Yes, he said all ye that hope in the Lord. You must hope and believe in the Lord. Yes, we must trust in him. Don't put your trust in man especially when things start to go bad. The first thought the devil put in our mind is where is your God now! Look at you all alone well I thought you said your God say he never leave you. Well yes, my God said he will never leave me nor forsaken me he said greater is him, that is in me than him that is in the world, and he said, that I am the temple of God. So that let us know that the God, that we serve he is our strength amen.

Now I'm getting ready to close this Chapter.

Now let us go to the gospel writer Matthew, before I get started, I will talk a little bit about the Savior, the Word of God that took on flesh came down from Heaven just to pay out our sinful debt that we couldn't pay out ourselves. He took the sins, of the whole entire world upon his shoulder just because he loves us and the thing about it when he came down here, he showed us, how to live on the words. And one thing we don't realize is, that what all he went through to get us saved. You see, even though he was in human flesh he was still yet all God. Because when he went to the Garden of Gethsemane, he knew, what he was about to Face by taking on the sins of the world, but he asked the father, is there any way that you can take this cup away from me. He is in the spiritual realm. He sees all and knows all. Just imagine for a moment taking the sins of the whole entire world upon his shoulder. The scripture say he was so stressful, that he starts to sweat blood! Now Medical Science says that man can sweat blood, but he will catch a heart attack or aneurism and he'll die. But you see the Word God Jesus Yashua couldn't die, because he was God in the flesh. He told the father nevertheless; thy will be done. When was the last time we told God let thy will be done. Because we always want things to go our way. We don't like to go through no pressure, but you see if God bring you to it, He will bring you through it, he never fails amen! Because he is a mighty God that we can trust in amen! Then he took that trip to the cross and they nailed him to the Cross. But before that they beat him up unrecognizable where his skin was torn apart just imagine that for a second. He did all that for us and he didn't complain, he did it because he loved us. He did it all because of the love that he had for us. Then they nail him to the Cross alive man just imagine the pain that he had to go through for us then they raised him up. I like that little slogan, if I be lifted, I'll draw all man onto me. Give him praise because that's what he did, he lifted it up for us hallelujah. Now when they lifted him up, he didn't complain. Remember he is the Word God and he could have called down a legion of angels to wipe everybody out. But he didn't do that, he said father forgive them because, they know not what they do? That is a merciful God. But before he gave up the Ghost, he said it was finished. Our debts was paid in full! Give him praise because he is so worthy to be praised amen and bless God. He did it all for us. Then they took him down and put him in a barrow tomb, why a barrow tomb? Because he was only there for a little while, three days and that was, it amens. Then when he rose, he stayed down here on earth for 40 days giving his disciples instruction for you and I today. Because we were on his mind Hallelujah! Then he went to his rightful place in heaven amen! That is a mighty God!

Now back to the scripture, the gospel writer Matthew Chapter 11 verse 28 through 30 This is the Messiah the Word speaking out to us Yashua better known as Jesus! He said come unto me all you that labor and are heavy laden and I will give you rest give you rest take my yoke upon you and learn of me; for I am meek and lonely in heart: and ye shall find rest unto your soul. For my Yoke is easy and my burden is light. Hallelujah gives Him praise! That is a mighty God that we serve! Amen and bless God.

Now I'm getting ready to close Chater 1 of (God Is My Everything!) Before I close, I must give some instruction especially in these latter days. The word of God is for all to get back to Him. Some people feel that have done too much, and feel it is too late to repent? It is not too late my brothers and sisters. All we must do is get up dust your clothes off, repent and get back into the game. Amen. I don't care what bad you have done on this Earth? You must trust in him. Amen.

Now we're going to go to Deuteronomy 31 verse 6 I got I must give some, instruction and the instruction are verse 6 says; Be strong that's the instruction, Be strong and of a good courage fear not, nor be afraid of them: for the Lord thy God, he it is that doth go with thee; God is letting us know that he is going to be with us, he'll never leave you.

Don't never let the devil put a thought in your mind and make you think that God is not there, God is with you especially, when you believe and trust in his words. He will not fail thee; God can't, fail amen. He will not fail thee, nor shall He forsake thee. The Mighty God that we serve will never leave us nor shall he ever forsake us. But we must believe, and trust in his words, apply yourself. I pray! Question? But are you applying yourself to the word of God are you trusting God with all your heart are, you being obedient? I know we none perfect we all make mistakes, but we got to believe and trust in God. When we fall get back up, repent because God, Jesus came and paid, all our sin out. He knows we human, he knows we make, Mistakes look at David was called man after God's Own Heart and David wasn't a perfect man amen, but he knows how to praise God! He would praise God for everything and gave all honor glory and praise unto God amen.

Now I'm getting ready to close as the question was at the beginning. Is the Lord our strength? and the answer; Yes, he is our shield and salvation. God's strength is made perfect in our weakness Hallelujah! as the Message was God Is Our Strength! Love you and God Love you more let's give Jesus a hand praise Glory. Hallelujah let's give him praise because he is so worthy to be praised amen, and bless God! (God Is Our Everything!)

7

CHAPTER TWO
God Will Make Away

Amen let's give Jesus a hand praise. Glory Hallelujah let's give him praise, because he is so worthy to be praised amen and bless God. First, I like to thank God for allowing us to be here on the Sabbath, day the holiest day of the week where our Lord have set aside and made the fourth Commandment that we keep this day holy amen.

Now let us go to God in prayers, oh gracious Eternal Father of Abraham, Isaac and Jacob, our father. Yahweh Elohim The Great I Am the creator, of the heavens and the Earth, Jehovah Jira our provider. Father God, we thank, you for being our provider Lord because we know by Your Word Lord God we can, stand strong because your word is true, and your word will not go out and come, back void. Father God, we ask you this day to decrease us and increase you, let it be all of you and none of us Lord allows us to take self and put self to the side this day Lord as you use us for your glory. Word our heart, minds and lips Lord Almighty. Keep us in your perfect will as we stand this day. Lord God, we Thank you for watching over us last night while we slept and Slumber. We thank, you Lord God for allowing nature to touch our eyes this day and awaken us to a brand new day, with a brand-new mercy, and a brand-new Grace. Father God we thank you for keeping your hand upon our kids, neighborhood, city, Parish, State Country and this wonderful world that you gave us to dwell in. Lord, we ask you to use us for your glory and we will be careful to make sure that we give you all the honor, all the glory and all the praise in Jesus most precious and holy name we pray amen and bless God.

Now I like to always ask God for message for you and I and why I always say I because we all came short of the glory of God the only perfect one that walked This Earth was the Messiah, the savior of the whole entire world. His name is. Jesus and without him where would we be? And God is so faithful to give us a Message.

9

Now I would like to start my introduction with a question. Is the Lord our strength? Most of us that have been through trials and errors of our life know that God had brought us to it, and he brought us through it Hallelujah. That is one thing about this Mighty God that we serve, if you believe and trust in him, he will bring us out of any situation that might seem impossible, but he is very able to do it amen. So, the answer is yes, he is our strength, shield and our Salvation. God Is Our Everything!

I like to always ask God for a blessing once again for you and me because we all need a blessing in these lateral days. And the blessing is may, God give us the power to trust, in him not man. That is why the scripture says trust in the Lord with all thine heart and lean not to your own understanding but in all thy ways acknowledge Him and He Shall direct your path. Let us give him praise! We can never give him enough praise, amen! God Is Our Everything!

I like to always say it in Jesus Christ holy name. There goes brother King again with that Jesus Christ Holy Name. Why in Jesus Christ Holy Name? Well, I'm glad you ask because in the gospel writer John 1 verse 1 say in the beginning was the word and the Word was with God. Now I like what the Messiah is the savior of the whole entire world. Sure, better known as Jesus said I am in my father and my father in I and he told, the disciples when you have seen me you have seen the father. Then the scripture says, the Word was God. That means the word took on flesh. Let's stop there for a second. If the word is God, that means he cannot lie? Because in the Book of Numbers chapter 23: 19 says God is not a man, that he should lie; neither the son of man, that he should repent: and verse 20 say he commanded to bless: and he hath blessed; and he cannot reverse it. So, that means whatever his word says he can't reverse it. God will not go against his word amen. And the Messiah the savior of the entire world the word of God Jesus says, anything hears me well anything you ask in my name it shall be given unto you by the Father which are in heaven. Let's give Jesus a hand praise. What do you need today my brothers and sisters, because God is able amen. Now that is enough introduction for today amen.

Now The Word Today is, God's strength is made perfect in our weakness. Let us go to our old Brother David in the Book of Psalms David the Book of Psalms chapter 73 verse 26 and we are going to see what our old Brother David had to talk about. Old David was from the Judah tribe. Judah was the son of Jacob. It reads in verse 26, My Flesh and my heart fail it, but God is the strength of my heart amen. God is the strength of my heart and my portion forever that means that God is our strength amen. Our brother David was telling us in that time and era that God is our strength amen. (God Is Our Everything!)

Let us go to Isaiah chapter 40 the prophet that prophesied about the Messiah coming and he came amen. Isaiah chapter 40 verse 31 And it reads, but they that waited upon the Lord shall renew, their strength: so that let us know God is our strength! We will renew our strength through the words of God. they shall Mount up with wings as eagles they shall run and not be weary and they shall walk and not faint. In other words, if we believe and trust in the Lord and we be obedient to his word God is going to be our strength amen.

Let us go to Isaiah chapter 41 verse 10, Hallelujah and I love what the Lord says to us repeatedly. Fear thou not; so that let us now when we serve a mighty God that, created Heaven and the Earth we shouldn't worry about nothing amen. Because there is nothing too hard for the God that we serve amen. He tells us, Don't worry about it just trust in him amen. So, it says; Fear thou not; for I am with thee; be not dismayed; for I am thy God: He is letting us know that he is our God when you trust in him and be obedient to his words amen. He said I will strengthen thee, God will, give us strength. God is our strength. (God Is Our Everything). I will help thee; I will uphold thee with thy right hand of my righteousness. Not man righteousness but God's righteousness amens.

Let us go to Second Corinthians chapter 12 verse 9; And he said unto me, my grace is sufficient for thee: for my strength is made perfect in weakness. Most gladly therefore will I rather glory in my infirmities, that the power of who of Christ may rest upon me. So, that let us know God is our strength and Our Everything amen.

Let us go back to old Brother David Hallelujah! Back to Psalms chapter 28 verse 7 and 8. I like our old Brother David, he wasn't perfect, but he was called a man after God's Own Heart. He knew how to praise God, that is the number one thing knowing how to praise God. Giving Him all the honor glory and praise. You see we have a problem right there; man, always want the glory every time they do something not knowing that God is allowing them to achieve in the things that we do. All the glory and honor go on to God amen. Because it is all about him the one that paid the price for us for our sins amen. Psalms 28 verse 7 through 8. The Lord is my strength. David let it be known that God is our strength, and my shield my heart does what trust in him you see, and I am helped therefore my heart greatly rejoice and with my song will I praise him. You see you got to give God all the praise because he is the one. Our life is already predestined, he made it possible. People love to say I did this, I did that, I made myself. No God made it possible for us to achieve in life. Verse 8 says; The Lord is the strength, and he is the saving strength of his anointed. Amen. (God Is Our Everything)

Let us go to Psalm chapter 31 verse 24. Be of good courage and he shall strengthen, your heart, all ye that hope in the Lord. (God is our strength and our Everything). He is the one that strengthen us, nobody else can do it, but God can. He will give you the ability to go through anything that you might have to face in life, and he is able to do it. You have got to hope, believe and trust in the Lord. Don't put your trust in man especially when things start to go bad. The first thought that the devil put in our mind is where is your God? Look at you now all alone. Well, I thought you said your God say he never leave you? Yes, my God said he will never leave me, nor forsaken me, he said greater is him, that is in me than him that is in the world, and he said that I am the temple

of God, So, that let us know that the God that we serve he is our strength.
(God Is Our Everything) amen.

Now I'm getting ready to close. Let us go to the gospel writer
Matthew. But before I close this chapter, I am going to talk a little bit
about the Savior, the Word of God that took on flesh and came down
from Heaven to pay out our sinful debt that we couldn't pay out
ourselves. He took the sins of the whole entire world upon his shoulder
just because he loves us and the thing about that is when he came down
here, he showed us how to live on the words. And one thing we don't
realize is that what all he had to go, through to get us save, you see even
though he was in human flesh he was still yet all God. Because when he
went to the Garden of Gethsemane, he knew what he was about to Face
taking on the sins of the world, but he asked the father is there any way
that you can take this cup away from me? He was in the spiritual realm;
he sees all and knows all. Just imagine for a moment taking the sins of
the whole entire world upon his shoulder. The scripture say he was so
stressful that he starts to sweat blood, now Medical Science says that man
can sweat blood, but he will catch a heart attack or aneurism or stroke
and die. But God the Word, Jesus, Yashua couldn't die unless give up the
ghost, because he was God in the flesh! But anyway, he told the father
nevertheless thy, will be done. When was the last time we told God let
thy will be done? Because we always want things to go our way, we don't
want to go through any pressure. But, if God bring you to it bring, he
will bring you through it. He never fails amen. Because he is a mighty
God that we can trust in amen! Then he took that trip to the cross, then
they nailed him to the Cross. But before that they beat him up
unrecognizable where his skin was torn apart, just imagine that for a
second. He did all that because of the love for us. And he did not
complain. Then they nail him to the Cross alive, just imagine the pain,
that he had to go through for us. Then they Rose him up, and I like that
little slogan say, if I be lifted up, I will draw all man onto me. Let's give
him praise. That is what he did, he was, lift it up for us hallelujah! Now
when they lifted him up, he did not complain. Remember he is God the
Word he could have called down a legion of angels to wipe everybody

out, but he did not do that instead he said, Father forgive them because they know not what do. That is merciful with much love. Then he said it was finished and gave up, The Ghost. It was done, our debts were paid in full! Give him praise because he is worthy to be praised amen and bless God. Yes, he did it all for us. Then they took him down and put him in a barrow tomb. Why a barrow tomb because he was only there for a little while, three days and that was it amen. Then when he rose, he stayed down here on Earth for 40 days giving his disciples instruction for us today because we were on his mind Hallelujah! Then he went to his rightful place in Heaven. Amen. That is a mighty God that we serve.

Back to the scripture the gospel writer Matthew 11 verse 28 through 30. This is the Messiah the Word of God speaking out to us Yashua better known as Jesus said, come unto me all ye that labor, that is a mighty God he said; and are heavy laden, I will give you rest. Take my yoke upon you and learn of me; for I am meek and lonely in heart: and ye shall find rest unto your souls. For my yoke is easy, and my burden is light. Hallelujah! Give Him praise! That is a Mighty God that we serve amen! Bless God!

Now I'm getting ready to close but before I close let me give you some instructions. I like to give some instruction especially in these latter days, because the word of God is for all of us. Some people feel that they have done too much and it's too late to repent. It is never too late as we have air to breathe my brothers and sisters. All we have to do is get up, repent and get back into the game amen. I don't care what bad you have done on this Earth. We got to trust in him amen.

Now let us go to Deuteronomy 31 verse 6. I must give some instructions. And the instruction is verse 6, Be strong and of good courage, fear not, (why should we fear if we are serving a mighty God) nor be afraid of them; for the Lord thy God, he is that doth go with thee; (God is letting us know that he's going to be with use) he will not fail thee, nor forsake thee. (He will never leave us, don't never let the devil put a thought in your mind and make you think that God is not there.

God is with you especially when you believe, and trust in his word. God cannot fail amen. The Mighty God that we serve he never leave us, nor shall he ever forsake us, but we just must believe and trust in his word. But I pray and nothing is happening to me. Question are you applying yourself to the words of God are you trusting God with all your heart are being obedient? I know we nonperfect because we all make mistakes, but we must believe and trust in God. When we fall, we must get back up and repent because God the Word, Yashua better known as Jesus came and paid all our sin out in full. He knew we humans would make mistakes. Look at David that was called man a man after God's Own Heart and David wasn't perfect. But he knows how to praise God. He would praise God for everything with all honor glory and praise unto God amen. Now I'm closing. As the question was at the beginning; Is the Lord our strength? And the answer was yes, he is our shield and salvation. God's strength is made perfect in our weakness. Hallelujah! And as the message was, God is our strength! I love you and God love you more let's. give Jesus a hand praise Glory Hallelujah let's give him praise because he's so worthy to be praised amen and bless God! (God Is Our Everything)

CHAPTER THREE
God Is in Control

Once again let's give Jesus' praise. Amen and bless God! Now first I like to thank God for allowing us to be here today on the Sabbath day the holiest day of the week where our God has commanded that we keep this day holy amen.

Every eye closed and let us pray. Oh, Eternal Father of Abraham, Isaac and Jacob our Father. The creator of the heavens and the Earth Jehovah Jira our Father. We come before you this day by your Grace obtaining Mercy making our request none unto you because your words are true and just. We ask you this morning as we come before you Lord decreases us and increase you, let it be all of you and none of us. Allow us to take selfies and put selfies to the side, while you use us to present your words to your people. We plead the blood of Jesus upon our kids, neighborhood, Parish, state our great Country that you have allowed us to do dwell and this wonderful world. Father God, we just thank you so much for all that you have doing. Because we know that your word say eyes have not seen nor ears heard nor enter in to the heart of man the things that God have for those who love him. Father God, we ask that you allow us to borrow your people's ears for a moment to present your word and we will be careful to give you all the honor glory and praise. In Jesus most precious and holy name we pray amen and bless God. Let's give Jesus another hand praise Hallelujah!

Now I like to always ask God for message once again for you and I. Why I say I because we all came short of the glory of God, there is only one perfect one that walk the Earth and that is the Messiah the savior of the whole entire world Yoshua better known as Jesus. And God is so faithful to give us a message when we ask for it.

But before I get started with the interdiction I would like to start with a question? Is God in control? Now remember the devil to work in our mind. We have 36,000 thoughts that runs through our mind daily, And the devil tries to put a thought in our minds to make us think God is not in control. The first thing he says is look at what's going on. Where is your God? That is when we must step up and say hold up, my God said he would never leave nor forsaken me. Then say the greater is him that is in me than him that is in the world. So, God is allowing things to happen to build up our faith because Faith pleases God with faith it is impossible to please God. So, God allowed him to do something and then we must shut the devil down through the words of God. The devil will back off if we keep applying ourselves to the word of God Amen!

And I like to always ask God for a blessing because we all need a blessing with all the things that is going on today the economy crash, the kids killing kids, all the troubles that is going on we need a blessing amen. And the blessing is may God give us the knowledge to understand his word and why I say? Because his words are true and justice. It will not go out and come back void, it's going to do exactly what it said is, going to do amen. I always like to seal it in Jesus Christ Holy name. Well, why in Jesus Christ's holy name? I am glad you asked, because in the Gospel writer John chapter 1 verse 1 says in the very beginning was the Word, (that came down from heaven) and the Word was with God, and I remember what the Messiah said I am in my Father and my Father in me, and when you have seen me you have seen me you have seen the Father, and then it says and the Word was God. Wait, stop there for a second. If the Word is God that means he cannot lie? So, it says in the Book of Numbers Chapter 23 verse 19. God is not a man to where he should lie. That let us know as we read the scriptures today is true. In the scriptures we going to talk about God being in control! That means all words are true and just. Keep that in your heart and your mind because the devil will try to erase those scriptures amen. Now the savior of the hold world Yashua better known as Jesus said, anything you ask in my name it shall be, not might be or maybe, but shall be given unto us by the Father which is in heaven. Let's give Jesus a hand praise because there's nothing too hard for the god that we serve amen. Now that's another introduction for today.

18

The Words Today are everything on Earth and in Heaven as it is written in Psalms chapter 24 verse 1 says, The Earth is the Lord's, and the fulness thereof; the world, and they that dwell therein. Everything belongs to God as I said earlier the rich the poor, everything belongs to God Amen. He said the world and they that dwelled there in everything belongs to God amen.

Now let us see what our brother Isaiah the prophet has to say about what God put on his heart to say in chapter 41 verse 10. Because remember Isaiah is the one that prophesied about the Messiah cometh and he came, the great counselor amens. Isaiah chapter 41 verse 10. Fear thou not; for I am with thee; be not dismayed; fore I am thy God: I will strengthen thee; yea, I will help thee; yea I will uphold thee with the right hand of my righteousness. (Well wait a minute, we are fearing because all the things that are going on in the world today, when the scripture is telling us fear not. We should not fear because we serve a great and Mighty God that is the creator of the heavens and the earth if we apply ourselves to his words, be obedient and be a doer of his words. We do not have to worry about all the things that is going on around us long as we put our belief and Trust in the Lord. God said he is with us, even if there is trouble all around us, he will protect us. Long as we are believers and a doer of his words. That is the sweet thing when we keep trying to do the right things which are to follow God's words in these trouble times coming against us. But it said if you be obedient, we are protected by God amen. Remember one thing, that his words are true and just. God will hold us with his right hand. I love what he says whom God holds in his hand no man can pluck him up amen! We serve a righteous and precious God amen.

Let us go to Proverbs, the book of wisdom King Solomon the son of King David, which David came from the tribe of Judah the fourth son of Jacob amen. Proverbs chapter 16 verse 4 through 9. Now we are going to read from the word of wisdom. The Lord hath made all things for himself; yea, why you worry God is in control? Yea even the wicked for the of evil. (God created all things). Every one that is proud in heart is an abomination (that means a lot of proud people in the world is in Abomination) to who the Lord; though hand join in hand, he shall not be unpunished. (He shall not be unpunished). Now listen at verse 6: By mercy and truth a iniquity is purged; and by the fear of the Lord men depart from evil. Verse 7 says; When a man way please the Lord, he maketh even his enemies to be at peace with him. That is a mighty thing Aman. Verse 8 says; Better is a little with righteousness than great revenues without right. (In other words what it is to have many things and not have no righteousness, that is bad). we cannot allow things to override our God when all the time we need him. Jesus is our life amen. Verse 9 says; A man's heart devises his way; but the Lord directed his steps. I love the word of God says the footsteps of a good man, is ordered by the Lord amen.

Now let us go to the Book of Job; now we know a lot about Job, He was a very noble man, but he had to go through some trials and tribulation and error of life. Now the scriptures never said that he wasn't going to go through troubles in life. It said many are the affliction of the righteous, but God will deliver us out them all praise God Amen and bless God.

Job chapter 42 verse 10. And the Lord turned the captivity of Job, when he prayed for his friends; also, the Lord gave Job twice as much he had before. But because of his faith and his trusting in God he was delivered out of his trials, tribulation and errors of life. Job was a rich man that lost it all. Because he kept the faith and belief, God delivered him out of his situations. Then God bless him with double of what he had before. So, as the same Godly servant today he says in Malachi chapter 3 verse 6 For I am the Lord, I change not. So, we must remember wherever we might be going through troubles or situations always stand on the word of God Amen. Always remember that God is in control don't worry about the things around us just keep believing, have faith and trust in God Amen.

Let us go to our old brother David in Psalms chapter 22 which was a man after God own heart amen and bless God. Verse 28 through 31. For the kingdom is the Lord's; and he is the governor among nations. (God is in control of everything). Verse 29 All they be fat upon earth shall eat and worship; all they that go down to the dust shall bow before him; and none can keep alive his own soul. (That let you know that God is in control)! Verse 30 says; A seed shall serve him; it shall be accounted to the Lord for a generation. Verse 31 says; They shall come and shall declare his righteousness unto a people that shall be born, (In other words God is in control forever and ever and ever more)! So, that means whenever our kids have kids it will go on from generations to generations. That his will be done. (God is in control)! It is done by him amen.

Let go to Psalms 115 verse 3. But our God is in the heavens; he hath done whatsoever he hath pleased. (Actually, nobody else but, God is in control). Sometimes the devil will try to put a thought in your mind and make you think that your God is not in control but always remember God is in control of everything amen.

Let us go to Isaiah chapter 45 verse 7. Here is the word that the Lord lead upon Isaiah's heart, and it let us know that God is in control. Remember whatever somebody tell us or whenever the devil tries to put a thought in our head, because the battle is in the mind. He trying to make you think that God is not in control. Well God is in control, and this is what the Lord told the prophet to say; I form the light, and create darkness: I make peace, and created evil: (God created Lucifer which is employed by God as a hit man when we out of line with God). I the Lord do all these things. Jesus the Messiah the savior of the whole entire world that pay our debt in full. So, whenever the devil put that thought in our mind saying, man it is too late in your life you cannot repent. That is a lie, it is he that can never repent. So, he tried to make you think that you cannot. Because he wants us to follow him. But because of what Jesus did for us we can get up, repent and get back in the game! God has made a way out of no way for us because he loves us. Nobody loves us like he does amen.

Now I'm getting ready to close, but I got to talk about our Messiah the savior of the whole entire world the Word that took on flesh, who came down from heaven because of the fall of Adam and Eve and took on the sins of the whole entire world he came down from heaven and when he came down before he went to the Cross he showed us how to live on the words God. Then before we went to the cross, he went down that path to be crucified. He was beaten unrecognizable, but he didn't complain because he knew he had a task because of the love that he has for every one of us today. Then after that he went to the cross and they nailed him alive to the cross, just imagine that for a moment being nailed to a cross. Yet, he still did not complain. Then they raise him up. Now remember he is the Word of God; he could have called a legion of angels down to wipe everybody out. But he knew that he was doing it for us. Then while he was hanging on the cross bleeding, he said Father forgive them because they do not know what they do. Now we see the physical trouble that he went through, but we couldn't see the spiritual trouble that he went through taking on the sins of the world since the time of Adam and Eve until now and the future. Just imagine billions and billions of people that came throughout this world. He was taken on by the sins of the whole entire world. We could not see the spiritual thing that was taking place. So, imagine how terrible that was. The Physical Realm was bad just imagine how tough tuff it was for him in while he was going through the spiritual realm Jesus cried with a loud voice, saying, Eli, Eli, Sabathani? My God, my God, why hast thou forsaken me? That was for every one of our sins. Jesus suffered for us because of the love he has for us.

All Because Of Love! Then he gave up on the ghost. Then they took him down from the cross and put him in a barrow tomb. Why do I say a barrow tomb? Because he only stays there for three days, just for a little while. Then he rose from that tomb, and he stayed on the earth for 40 days giving his disciples instruction for us today! That let us know that the Lord is still in control today. Give Jesus a praise. Hallelujah! God is still in control! God loves us more than anybody else could ever love us on this Earth. His love is shall all over us as we speak. now I'm getting ready to close I'm close in Ephesians chapter 1 verse 11 and 12. In whom also we have obtained an inheritance, being predestinated according to the purpose of him who worketh all things after the counsel of his own will: We must remember our life is already predestinated. God already know everything about us. He is the Alpha and the Omega, the beginning and the end. He knows the ending before the beginning. So, he already knows what's going to go on in our life the next second, hour, day, month, year and the ending predestinated according to the purpose of him who walks all things after the concept of his own will. God's will not men will amen. Verse 12 says: That we should be to the praise of his glory, who first trusted in Christ.

Now I have just finished telling you the story about the Messiah the Savior of the whole entire world Yashua better known as Jesus. He did it all for us, my brothers and sisters. And he is still in control today! Anytime you are going through something don't never let the devil put a thought in your mind and say God is not in control. God said in his words, he would never leave us, nor shall he ever have forsaken us. He will always be there because he's the greatest him that is in you than him that is in the world. When the devil put a thought in your mind when trouble start, pull down that stronghold and call on Jesus. Continua being obedient to him and always remembering I don't give a care how bad your sins are, do not let the devil tell you it is all over, you have done too much, you cannot repent. Tell the devil he is a Liar. All we must do is repent and turn away from sin. God already told us in second Chronicles chapter 7 verse 14. If my people, (God's peoples) which are called by my name, shall humble themselves, and pray and seek my face, and turn from their wicked ways; then will I hear from heaven, and will forgive their sin, and heal their land. If we would just follow God's instruction the violence and hatred would stop, then love would step in. If we could only learn to follow the word of God how happy we would be. And do what God tell us to do, he will hear from heaven and heal our land and forgive our sins. Give him praise Glory Hallelujah! As the question was at the very beginning, I'm closing now. Is God in control?

Answer is yes, God is in control. I love you and God love you more! let's give Jesus' praise amen and bless God.

CHAPTER FOUR
We Need God's Grace

Amen let's give Jesus a hand praise Glory Hallelujah let's give him praise amen and bless God. First, I want to thank God for giving us another day to worship him on the Sabbath day the holiest day of the week where our Lord and savior have commanded the fourth Commandment to keep this day holy amen and bless God.

Now let us go to God in Prayers. Every head bows every eye closed. Gracious Eternal Father of Abraham, Isaac and Jacob, Abba Father Yahweh Elohim the Great I Am, the creator of the heavens and earth, Jehovah Jireh our provider. Yes, Lord we know that you are our provider and we come boldly to you your throne of grace obtaining Mercy making our requests known unto you because your words say we received not because we ack not, but we ask the Lord that you give us wisdom knowledge and understanding to be obedient to your word. To be a doer of your word, Lord we plead the blood of Jesus upon our kids, neighborhoods, city, Parish, State, great country that we dwell in and this wonderful world that you have given us to live in. We know that there is nothing too hard for the God that we serve. Lord, we thank you so much for all that you have been doing by allowing us to have air to breathe, allowing nature to touch our eyes and awaken us. Father God you are awesome, and we thank. We give you all the honor, glory and praise in Jesus most precious and Holy Name amen and bless God. Let's give him praise. Glory Hallelujah let's give him praise because he's so worthy to be praise amen and bless God.

Now I like to always ask God for a message for you and I and why I always say I because we all came short of the glory of God. The only perfect one that walked the earth was the Messiah the savior of the whole world, Yeshua better known as Jesus. Yes, he came down here and walked the street and was the only perfect one amens. He is always faithful to give us a word amen.

25

So, I would like to start the introduction off with a question. The question is do we need God's, Grace? The answer is yes because we all came short of the glory of God. We need the gift of Grace.

I'm going to be talking about our brother Paul that ask God about the thorn in his side. That means whatever troubles that you might be going through that is your thorn in your side. Paul asked God to remove it. You see many of times we're going through problems we always asking God to please remove it, but we do not realize that God allowing us to go through it. So that when we come out of our trials and tribulation there is going to be a blessing waiting for us amen. Yes, indeed so, the message that God laid upon my heart is; We Need God's Grace!

Now I always like to ask God for a blessing once again for you and I, because we all need a blessing of from God Amen. The blessing is may, God give us the gift of grace through faith. Well brother King why faith? Because Faith pleases God, without it is impossible to please God. So, we must have Grace through faith amen. So, I like to always seal it in Jesus Christ's holy name amen. Okay brother King there you go again in Jesus Christ holy name. Why in Jesus Christ's holy name? Well I'm glad you asked because in the gospel writer John chapter 1 verse 1 says; in the beginning in the very beginning was the Word and the Word was with God, (and I love what the Messiah said Yashua better known as Jesus said I am in my Father and my Father in me and when you have seen me you have seen the Father amen), and the Word was God. Okay let's put bricks on for a minute right there. If the Word is God that took on flesh, that means he cannot lie? Because in the Book of Numbers Chapter 23 verse 19 say God is not a man to where he should lie. You see man always lying, he makes promises that he cannot keep. Nor son of man to where he should repent. Verse 20 say; God commanded a blessing, (you see God command his word to do what he said it is going to do) he command a blessing and he cannot reverse it. That is the wonderful God that we serve. So, the Word the Messiah, Yeshua better known that Jesus said; anything (hear me well) anything you ask in my name it shall be, not might be or maybe, but shall be given, On To You by The Father Which is in Heaven. Give Jesus our Lord praise. Hallelujah Because he's so worthy to be praise amen and bless God.

Now that's enough introduction for today now let us go to The Words Today. The word today is God gift of Grace is what we need in these troubled times! Now we are going see what the second Corinthians chapter 12 verse 7 through 9 must talk about. We will be talking about our older brother Paul verse 7. Any lest I should be exalted above measures through the abundance of the revelations, there was given to me a thorn in the flesh, (in other words that could be whatever the trouble you are going through that could be your Thorn In the Flesh) the messenger of Satan to buffet me, (that means whatever trouble it was brought through by Satan to buffer me) lest I should be exalted above measure.

Verse 8 says; For this thing I besought the Lord thrice, (in other words three times he besought the Lord to take the trouble away from him. Like I was saying earlier we know many times when we have trouble we cry out, oh Lord why me why am I going through this situation. But we don't realize that God allowing it to happen so, in other words he brought us to it so he can bring us through it. The thing about that is when we get out of that situation that we are going through you can straighten your brothers. We can tell them; look don't worry about it just trust in God. Because if he did it for me, he would do it for you amen.

He said I said, but for this thing I besought the Lord Thrice (three times) that it might be, departed from me. He wanted that trouble, whatever that thorn was that he was going through he wanted it to be over with. Verse 9 said: And he said unto me, my grace is sufficient for thee; (in other words we need God's grace. The Lord was speaking to Paul at the time, and he was telling him my grace is sufficient. So, all we must do is do not be concerned about what we are going through, we must realize that God's grace is sufficient.) for my strength is made perfect in weakness. (In other words when we are weak God is strong amen. So, Grace will get us through our situation through faith. Some people may ask the question; how do I get Grace? The answer to that is through faith. Why faith brother King? Because Faith pleases God. With out Faith it is impossible to please God Amen.) Most gladly therefore will I rather glory in my infirmities, that the power of Christ May rest me.

Let us go to the book of Ephesians chapter 2 verse 8 and 9. Remember we need God's grace in a time like now with all the trials, tribulation and errors of life that is going on. We need God's grace because grace is going to get us through our situation by Faith amen.

Ephesians chapter 2 verse 8 says for the grace through faith (that is how you receive grace through faith) he said and that not of yourself (you see a lot of times we think we could achieve things on our own but it's through God's grace and then how we receive that grace through faith amen) is it in that not of yourself it is the one the gift of God. Grace is a gift of God that you receive through faith amen. None of your works, this what we say; I did this myself; I went through the situation myself, nobody else did It but me myself and no that is a lie, there is no truth. It is through God's grace through faith. There is not any man to boast, so that means; that you should not boast about what you, doing. You should boast about what God is doing amen.

Let us go to James chapter 4 verse 6. But we giveth more grace, (God giveth more grace) wherefore he saith, God resisted the proud, (that is the one thinks they are doing all these things themselves saying that it wasn't God, but it was what I did. No that is a lie and there's no truth in it. He said, but God giving Grace onto the humble. Yes, he does, that is what I love about God.

Second Chronicles chapter 7 verse 14 say: If my people, which are called by my name, shall humble themselves, and prey, and seek my face, and turn from their wicked ways; then will I hear from heaven, and will forgive their sin, and will heal their land. (That is why the gift of Grace goes onto the humble, you got to humble yourself amen.)

Let us go to First Corinthians chapter 15 verse 10. But by the grace of God, I am what I am: (God's grace is what you are not by yourself, everything that you achieve is because of God's grace that allow you to go through whatever you have gone through. Whatever your troubles are situations might be). You know it's because of God's grace I am what I am, and you are who you are through the grace of God and his grace which was bestowed, upon me was not in vain; but I labored more abundantly than they are: yet not I, but the grace of God which was with me. (That is how I achieved what I achieved, who I am what I am, and who you are who you are. Because of the grace of God. We need the grace of God in these troubled times that we are going through. We need the grace of God Amen.

Let us go to Titus Chapter 2 verse 11 through 14. For the grace of God that bringeth salvation hath appeared to all man. (The grace of God brings salvation and had appeared to all men. We need God's grace.) Verse 12 Teaching us that, denying ungodliness and worldly lust, we should live soberly, righteously, and godly, in this present world; (that's some of the things that we should do to achieve Grace by following God's instructions.) Verse 13. Looking for that blessed hope, and the glorious appearing of the great God and our Savior Jesus Christ; (The same one the Word that took on flesh, that came from Shekinah glory amen.)

Verse 14. Who gave himself for us, that he might redeem us from all iniquity and purify unto himself a peculiar people, zealous of good works. (All through our Lord and savior the Word himself Yeshua better known as Jesus in the English language; we need God's grace amen.)

Let us go to Romans chapter 3 verse 20 through 24. Therefore, by the deeds of the law there shall no flesh be justified in his sight: for by the law is the knowledge of sin. (The law shows us the things that we should not do.)

Verse 21. But now the righteous of God without the law is manifested, being witnessed by the law and the prophets.

Verse 22. Even the righteousness of God which is by faith (Faith remember through faith that's how we receive Grace) of Jesus Christ unto all and upon all them that believe: (remember we must believe and cannot doubt the word of God.)
there is no difference:

Verse 23. For all have sinned, (Let us stop there for a second, you know there's a lot of great brothers and sisters today think that they are not a sinner. Now remember we done already clarify the word of God cannot lie and here are the word of God telling us for all have sinned and came short of the glory of God. That means all Humanity has sinned.) and come short of the glory of God.

Verse 24. Being justified freely by his grace (not ours but God's grace) through the redemption that is in Christ Jesus: (That is in Christ Jesus, we must remember that Jesus Paid the price amen.)

Now I'm getting close to closing. We must remember we need God's grace in the times that we are going through. We all know that all these things that's going on in the world, kids killing kids, wars and rumors of wars, earthquakes and divers' plays, floods, Famine, economy crashing. We all see these things going on today. We need God's grace amen.

Let us go to Romans chapter 5 verse 8. But first, I must tell you about Our Lord and savior the Word which was in Heaven. He took on the job as Savior of the world when Adam felt, then he came down from Heaven took on flesh and showed us how to live on the word of God. Then he took on the sins of the whole entire world from the time of Adam and Eve to the present where we live and into the future. He took on the sins of Every Soul That Ever Walked on the Earth who wanted to get saved. He was crucified, Beat, spit on, ridiculed, because he was paying our sinful debt in full. Nobody else could have paid for it but him. Then he was nailed to the cross, can you imagine it he was alive, and he was nailed to the cross. Then he was lifted. I like that old saying if I be lifted, I will draw all men onto me. That is what he did draw all men. All that was happening to him he said Father forgive them because they know not what they do. They did not know that they were destroying their own savior. That was a task that he had taken on to save the whole world from sins. Then he was put in a borrower tomb. Why a borrow tomb, because he only stayed there for three days, just for a little while. Then he rose, but before he left earth, he stayed there for 40 days to give his disciples instructions, to give to us today. Then he left and went to his rightful place in Heaven. This was all done because he loves us. When he laid down his life for his friend the sinners amen.

I am getting ready to close. Romans chapter 5 verse 8, 9. But God commanded his love towards us, that, while we were yet sinners, Christ died for us. (Nobody loves us like God loves us. He commanded his love towards us while we were yet sinners. Christ died for us he did it for us paid out our sinful debt for us that we may have a taste of the Tree of Life.)

Verse 9. Much more then, being now justified by his blood, we shall be saved from wrath through him. Oh my God that is wonderful to know that we are saved from the Wrath through him amen. God is so good.

I am going to close now in Isaiah the prophet. Isaiah chapter 40 verse 31. Always remember we need God's grace through these times that we are going through in the world today.

Let us go to Isaiah chapter 40 verse 31. Now remember Isaiah was the one prophesied about the Messiah coming and he came. Verse 31. But they then wait upon the Lord shall renew their strength; they shall mount up with wings as eagles; they shall run, and not be weary; and they shall walk, and not faint. (Wait upon the Lord. We do not want to wait upon the Lord. Do not have time for God, we want to take God and put him on the back burner. When all the time we need him. I love what the word of God said, if we draw nigh to him, he draws nigh to us, whom God holds in his hands no man can pluck us out, if God be for us who or what can be against us, and no weapon form against us all prosper. Give God praise Hallelujah amen and bless God. When you wait upon the Lord, not upon yourself, not upon man, we shall run and not be weary, no you do not have to worry about nothing when they should run and not be weary, they shall walk and not faint. All we must do is learn how to stand, on God's words at a time like now my brothers and sisters. If we want to make it through this, we are going to have to follow God's instructions. There is no other way, but through Jesus the Word himself he is the right to the heaven. So, we need God's grace amen. And in closing the question was Do We Need God's grace? The answer is yes, we need God's grace, it is a gift of God. That is what we need in the trouble times, that we are going through right now. As the message was; We Need God's Grace! I love you and God love you more! Let's give Jesus a hand praise Hallelujah amen and bless God.

CHAPTER FIVE
God Is Our Protector

Amen let's give Jesus [Applause] amen and bless God. First, I'd like to thank God for allowing us to be here today on the Sabbath day the holiest day of the week for our Lord has anointed and appointed for us to sub with him.

Now every head bow and let us go to God in prayer! Oh, Eternal Father of Abraham, Isaac and Jacob. Father Yahweh Elohim the Great I Am, the creator of the heavens and the Earth, Jehovah Jari, our provide. Yes, and we thank you for allowing us to be here before you today. Lord, we thank you for allowing nature to touch our eyes and awaken us on this day. We ask that you continue to order our footsteps Lord God Almighty. Decrease us and increase you let it be all to you and none of us. Allows us to bring forward your word to your people Father God. We give you honor, glory and praise. In Jesus most precious and holy name amen.

I always like to ask God for message once again for you and me. Why I always say I because we all come short of the glory of God. The only perfect one that walk the earth is our Lord savior, Yashua better known as Jesus. Because we all need a word from God amen.

But now before I get started, I would like to ask a question. Is God our protector? Well, most of us brothers and sisters that have been through life know that God has brought us to it and brought us through it. We know that he is our protector because it was not the things that we had done that brought us through it. But what he did and is still doing for us today. If you have never experienced anything yet well, you have not experienced life yet. Look out because it is coming amen. And the answer is he is our protector and there is no weapon formed against us shall prosper amen. Whom God hold in his hand no man can us out, if

God be for us who can be against us amen. So, God lead on my heart. The message is God is our protector! Yes, he is.

I would like to ask Lord for blessing for you and I because we all need a blessing in a time like now. We know there are a lot of things that are going on in the world today. This is the hour and the time that we need to get closer to God amen. And the blessing is my God keep his unchanging hands upon us because God don't change. It is written; I'm the Lord thy God and I change not. God do not change amen. I like to always seal it in Jesus Christ holy name amen. Okay brother King there you go again in Jesus Christ Holy Name. Yes, I'm going to keep repeating it repeatedly. That is why I like Jeremiah, which I called the weeping prophet. Why, because he used to cry out for God peoples trying to let us know that the hour is now amen. So that is what I'm doing now I'm crying out to let them know that it is time to call on that mighty name Jesus Christ Holy Name amen. Why Jesus Christ Holy Name? Well, I am glad you asked. Because it is written; in the gospel writer John chapter 1 verse 1 in the beginning in the very beginning was the word, the word was in heaven and the Word was with God. And I love, what the Messiah Yashua better known as Jesus said; I am in my Father and my Father in me, and when you have seen me, you have seen the Father. So, we know now that Jesus is the Messiah, and we need to call upon him. And it is written; The Word was God. Let us pause for a moment right there. If the word is God that means he cannot lie? Because the Book of Numbers Chapter 23 verse 19 read; God is not a man to where he should lie nor the son of man to where he should repent. So that let us know that God cannot lie. It is written in Verse 20 that God commanded a blessing, and he cannot reverse it. So, that means if God says something that's what it is. God do not change for nobody. So as the Messiah, Yashua better known as Jesus said; anything you ask in my name it shall be given unto us by the Father which are in heaven. Now let us give Jesus a hand praise amens and bless God. Now that is enough introduction for today amen.

Now the word today is when we follow God's words his truth shall be our Shield and buckler. Now we are going go to Psalms 91. We are going to hear what our old Brother David had to talk about it because David was call a man after God own heart. He was not perfect; he made some mistakes, but he knew how to cry out to God. You know one thing I like about David is he knew how to praise God constantly. He had a personal relationship with God. We need to learn how to have a personal relationship with God. That is what we truly need amen.

Now we are going to see what old David must talk about Psalms 91 verse 3 through 7. That's what I like about David he knows how to cry out to God, and he let God know how he felt about him amen.

Now it reads in verse 3; Surely, he shall deliver thee, God will deliver us if we be obedient, and be a doer of his word God. (He is our protector) from the snare of the fowler, and from the noisome pestilence.

Verse 4. He shall cover thee (that let us know he's going to protect us through all our situation) with his feathers, and under his wings shalt thou trust; his truth shall be thy shield and buckler. (That is a mighty God who let us know that he is going to protect us)

Verse 5. Thou shalt not be afraid for the terror by night; nor for the arrow that flieth by day; (That is the word of God my brothers and sister he tells us all through the Bible fear not, because he is a might God that we serve that will meet our needs and protect us.)

Verse 6 reads; Nor for the pestilence that walketh in darkness; nor for the destruction that wasted at noonday.

Verse 7 reads; A thousand shall fall at thy side, and ten thousand at thy right hand. But it shall not come nigh thee. (Let us give him Praise because that let us know that God is our protector amen.)

Now let us go to Proverbs, the book of wisdom. We are going see what our brother, Solomon had to talk about. Remember Solomon was son of David which from Jacob, the Judah tribe the fourth son of Jacob amen.

Proverbs 18 verse 10. the Book of wisdom reads; The name of the Lord is a strong power: the righteous runneth into it, and safe. (In other words when we call upon the name of the Lord we can run into that tower of protection and be safe. We are covered by the blood.)

God got his hand upon us if we been obedient and being a doer of his word amen.

Let us go to the book of Exodus and see what God laid our old brother Moses to talk about. Exodus chapter 23 verse 25. And ye shall serve the Lord your God, and he shall bless thy bread, and thy water; and I will take sickness away from the midst of thee. (God will be our protector, he will take our sickness away from us amen.)

Let us go to the book of Philippians. I'm just running through a few things that God wants us to know at a time like now. Because we know that we are living in trouble times. It was foretold in the scriptures in the days of old that this was going to be like the days of Noah. In the days of Noah, it was very wicked and right now the world we live in is very wicked. People killing people for simple thing. I don't like the way you look at me, I don't like the clothes you wear, I don't like what you said to me. But what did I say, all I said was Jesus love you, and that is true amen.

Philippians chapter 4 verse 13 reads; I can do what all things through Christ which strengthened me. (We do not have to worry about anything when we are serving God. He is our protector; he will bring us through our troubles. Now once we get saved, we have a thing about being a believer that nothing is going to happen to us, but we have got to remember what the scripture tells us. God did not say that nothing was going to happen. Because the scripture said many are the Affliction of the righteous, but the sweet thing of it is he will deliver us out of them all amen and bless God.)

Now let us go to the book of Isaiah the prophet, the one that prophesied about the Messiah is coming and he came the comforter our great counselor amen.

Isaiah chapter 54 verse 17 and these are the words that the Lord spoke through Isaiah, and it reads verse 17. No weapon that is formed against thee shall prosper; and every tongue that shall rise against thee in judgment thou shalt condemn. This is the heritage of the servants of the Lord, and their righteousness is of me, saith the Lord. (So, no weapon that form against the gospel shall prosper. So, whatever the devil got in his mind he is just wasting his time because we already got the victory when Jesus went to the cross amen. This is the heritage of the servants of God.) Remember we said earlier that God cannot lie right? If he cannot lie well that means his words are true. So, if it tells us, we must believe that. We must trust in him. I am not saying to go and run across the street and hit somebody in the head no, but believe and trust God's words, love each other as he first loves us. Then we do not have anything to worry about. Just be obedient and a doer of his word follow his instructions. The only thing that we can stand in this world is the foundation is the word of God amen.

Let us go to Hebrews chapter 13 verse 6. So that we may boldly say, The Lord is my helper, and I will not fear what man shall do unto me. (Remember even your enemy belongs to God. Don't you know your enemy can't do nothing unless God allow him to. Lucifer cannot do anything to us unless God allowed him to do it. So, God is let us know that he is our helper in a time of need, and he is our protector.) Then he said and I will not fear what man should do unto me, we do not have to worry about a man, if we are being obedient to God, and if you know that we are his children by being a servant of his by being obedient to his word and being a doer of his words. We do not have to worry about a thing. That is why the word of God of says fear not over again. God is our protector amen. Now I'm getting ready to close this chapter.

Deuteronomy in the Old Testament, Deuteronomy chapter 31 verse 6. Now God is going to give us some instructions telling us what to do at a time like now. Because we know that God's words cannot lie. We must believe this in our heart, God say we must trust his words. That is the only thing in this world we can trust, we cannot trust anybody else. A lot of men make promises they cannot keep saying, I will do this, or I will do that. But when the time comes, he says Brothers or Sisters I'm sorry, but something came up. There are always excuses. But God word is true and just. It will what is said it will do when we apply ourselves to his words. And those of us that have been through trials and tribulations in life know that when we call on God, he has delivered us out of situation where no man could have gotten us out but only God amen.

Deuteronomy chapter 31 verse 6 reads; Be strong and of good courage, fear not, nor be afraid of them: for the Lord thy God, he it is that doth go with thee; he will not fail thee, nor forsake thee. (So, be strong and of good cheer because the fact is we know the Mighty God, the Creator is well able to protect us. He said fear not nor be afraid of them, for the Lord thy God he is that did go with thee.

God has done so much for us. The Word had to come down from Heaven the lord was in heaven and then the Word came down and took on flesh amen. He didn't have to do this, but it is because of the love that he had for us. Remember Adam and Eve fell and when they felt he could have started humanity all over again. But he has so much love for Humanity that he came down to Earth because he wasn't going to go against his word. That let us know that his words are true and just. Then the Word the flesh came down here and he shows how to live on his word. The Messiah the savior of the hold world paid out our debt in full, he was beaten, ridiculed spit on and he didn't say anything because he came for a purpose. He could not go against his word, so he came down here to pay for our sins in full. Then he went to the cross and he was nailed alive to the cross just imagine for a moment. And he did it because of the love that he had for us. He paid that price out in full, and then the thing about it was when he hung on the cross, he cried up to the father to forgive them because they know not what they do. Then when they took him down, they put him in a barrowed tome. Why I say a barrow tome because he was only in there for three days a short period of time. Then he rose and stayed on Earth 40 days and gave his disciples some instructions on what to do for us from generation to generation to let us know what to do at a time like now. Then went to heaven in his rightful place. He did it all because he loved us.

And as he was telling in Deuteronomy chapter 31, he said be strong, we got to be strong, and of good courage and then it says fear not be not afraid of them for the Lord thy God he is with thee. God will not fail, whatever his words said it is going to do.

Remember he lives in us; he loved us first and he said he would never us nor forsake us. All we must do is trust in him. Trust in the Lord with all your heart and lean not to your own understanding. You see that part about understanding, devil the Battleground is in our mind and he try to put a thought in our minds to make us think that our God do not love us which God has already shared with us. I just told the story of what Jesus did for us the Word that came from Heaven. You see he tried to put that thought in our mind and make us think that our God cannot prevail. But we must believe and trust in God. But in all God's ways acknowledge Him and he shall direct our path. Let us give him praise. Glory Hallelujah!

CHAPTER SIX
God Will Meet Our Needs

Let us give Jesus a hand praise amen and bless God. First, I would like to thank God for allowing us to be here today on the Sabbath day the holiest day of the week where our God has made the fourth Commandment to keep this day holy amen.

Now let us go to God in prayers. Every eye closed, every head bowed. Oh, Gracious Eternal Father of Abraham, Isaac and Jacob, Our Father Yahweh, Elohim, The Great I Am, the creator of the heaven and the earth. Lord you are our provider, and we thank you for this brand-new day with a brand-new Mercy and a brand-new Grace. Lord, we ask you to continue to keep your hands upon us. The Lord gives us wisdom, knowledge and understanding as we get ready to break the bread of life with your people. Lord, we ask you to use us like you never used us before. Lord decreases us and increase you let it be all of you and none of us. Allow us to take self and put self to the side. Have your way Lord and let thy will be done not our way Lord. We thank you Lord Father God, we give you honor, we give you glory, we give you praise. In Jesus most precious and holy name we pray amen and bless God. Let us give Jesus another hand praise.

Now I would like to ask God for a message once again for you and I. Because we all need a word from God especially in these lateral days that we are going through right now. The devil is having him a great old time right now. So, now we need to get closer to God and we need a word from God Amen. He is always so faithful to give us a word. But now before we get started, I always like to ask a question? When we follow God's instruction will he meet our needs? You see we have a problem right there; we always like to follow man's instructions and man always make promises that he cannot keep. Man changes, but God I never change. So, the answer to that question is yes, he will meet our needs. We always look at blessing as being finances but what it is to be a rich

41

man and do not have any legs to walk on amen? What it is to be rich and have bad health? Seeing money cannot buy health. So, we need those blessings from God amen. God can meet our need whatever we might be going through God can meet our needs amen.

So, the message that God laid upon my heart is God Will Meet Our Needs! Amen. Now I like to always ask God for a blessing for you and I. And the blessing is May God meet our needs not our greed. You see the thing about that is as soon as God open the door of blessings we ask for a place of business, mansion, a big fat bank roll and many material things. But never asking God for the spiritual gifts that is going to lead us to godly things and direct us in life. So, the blessing that He laid upon my heart is, to meet our needs not our greed's. I always like to seal it in Jesus Christ holy name amen. Okay there go brother King again with that Jesus Christ Holy Name. Yes, I'm going to keep on, repeating it over again because we need Jesus in a time like now. Well okay brother King, why is Jesus Christ Holy Name? Well, I am glad you asked. It reads in the gospel writer John chapter 1 verse 1 reads in the beginning was the Word and the Word was with God, and I like what the Messiah the saver of the whole entire world Yeshua in the Hebrew language and Jesus in the English language said I am in my father and my father in me. And he told his disciples when you have seen me you have seen the father. Then the word of God was God. We'll put on brakes right there for a moment. Now if the Word is God the Word that took on flesh which is Jesus, that means he cannot lie. So, as we read the scriptures today that let us know that his word will not go out and come back void. It is going to do exactly what it said it is going to do.

So, the Book of Numbers Chapter 23 verse 19 reads God is not a man, that he should lie; neither the son of man, that he should repeat: So, that let us know now that God cannot lie amen. Now Yashua better known as Jesus in the English language said anything you ask in my name it shall be, not may be, or might be, but it shall be given on to you by The Father, which are in heaven, let us give Jesus a hand praise. Hallelujah! Now that is enough introduction for today amen.

Now let us go to The Words Today. And the words today are when we follow God's instruction which is his word, he will meet our needs not greed's. So, what do you need today, my brothers and sisters? There is nothing too hard for the God that we serve. He will meet all our needs.

Let us read what Philippians chapter 4 verse 19 have to say about our needs. Remember that words of God are true and just, it will not go out and come back void. It is going to do exactly what he said it is going to do, if we apply ourselves to his words amen.

Verse 19 reads; But my God shall supply all your need according to his riches in glory by Christ Jesus. (The Messiah the savior of the whole entire world The Word that took on
flesh amen.)

Let us go to Psalms chapter 37 verse 3 through 6. We are going to see what our old Brother David talk about. The scriptures say David was a man after God's Own Heart. He was from Jacob fourth son Judah tribe. David knew how to cry out to God; he knew how to praise God amen. He was not perfect he made many mistakes, but he knew how to plead out to God amen.

Psalms chapter 37 verse 3 through 6. (Brother David is giving us some instructions.) Verse 3. Trust in the Lord, and do good; so shalt thou dwell in the land, and verily thou shalt be fed. (God will meet our need, Brother David has let us know that God will meet hour need if we apply ourselves by trusting in the Lord and His words.)

Verse 4. Delight thyself also in the Lord, and he shall give thee the desires of thine heart. (God is letting us know that he will meet our needs through his words. Just follow God's instruction and He will give us the desires of our hearts.)

Verse 5. Commit thy way unto the Lord; (He is telling us to give ourselves to the Lord, surrender ourselves over to Him.) trust also in him; (That means put our trust in God.) and he shall bring it to pass. Amen. (Whatever you need God will bring it to pass if we apply ourselves by trusting in the Lord, being obedient to his word and being a doer of his word.)

Verse 6. And he shall bring forth thy righteousness as the light, and thy judgment as the noonday. (Brother David is letting us know that it is time to get our house in order and how to praise God in these trouble times. We need to trust God and His words.

Let us go to Psalms chapter 23. That is one of the old favorite scriptures I have been hearing years since I was a little boy. A very familiar passage of scriptures that many have written on the table of their hearts. This is what David was saying.

Psalm chapter 23 verse 1 through 6. The Lord is my shepherd, I shall not want.

Verse 2. He maketh me to lie down in green pastures: (God make our place comfortable) he leadeth me beside the still waters. (When we are sitting around still waters it looks so calm and peaceful, giving you peace of mind.)

Verse 3. He restoreth my soul he leadeth me in the paths of righteousness for his name's sake. (Not for man but for his name's sake.)

Verse 4. Yea, though I walk through the valley of the shadow of death. I will fear no evil: (Why should we worry when we serve a mighty God that oversees everything. He still sits on the throne, and he will meet our needs.) for thou art with me; thy rod and thy staff they comfort me. (Peace, God will comfort us in the mist of our troubles.)

Verse 5. Thou preparest a table before me in the presence of mine enemies: (All our enemy can do is sit and watch us be blessed.) thou anoints my head with oil; my cup runneth over.

Verse 6. Surely goodness and mercy shall follow me all the days of my life; and I will dwell in the house of the Lord forever. (That is a Mighty God we serve Amen.) We should be giving Him Praise. Glory Hallelujah amen and blessed God.

Let us go to Matthew chapter 7 verse 7 through 11. God will meet our needs, all we got to do is be obedient, a doer of his words and follow his instruction amen. This is what our Lord and savior said.

Verse 7. Ask, and it shall be given you; seek, and ye shall find; knock, and it shall be opened unto you: (Ask, Seek, and Knock, that is what we supposed. The scriptures says, Seek ye first the kingdom of God and his righteousness and all these things shall be added unto you. So that let us know that God will meet our needs.

Verse 8. For everyone that asked received; and he that seeking fined; and to him that knocked it shall be opened. (God will open those doors where man has closes. He will meet our needs.)

Verse 9. Or what man is there of you, whom if his son ask bread, will he give him a stone? (Now we who love our children know if they ask for a piece of bread, you want to give them a stone. That is our children, we love them.)

Verse 10. Or if he asks a fish, will he give him a serpent? (If our kids ask for a fish, we want to give him a snake.)

Verse 11. If ye then being evil, know how to give good gifts unto your children, how much more shall your Father which is in heaven give good things to them that ask him? (This is our Mighty Father that we are serving today which is in heaven. He is going to meet all our ever and any needs. The moral of the story is what are your needs today? Because God can meet your needs amen.)

Let us turn to the book of Hebrews chapter 4 verse 16. Let us therefore come boldly unto the throne of grace, (I like what Apostle Paul said about Jesus, he is the grace of grace amen.) that we may obtain mercy and find grace to help in time of need. (God will meet our needs. The scriptures are telling us brothers the sisters when we apply, ourselves to the word of God, be obedient and a doer of his words meaning when we follow his instructions, not man because man can always let us down and make us promises that he cannot keep. If God say it, he will do it when we apply ourselves to his word amen.) I'm getting ready to close this chapter.

Let us go to the Book of Exodus the Old Testament and see what it says not only will He meet our needs, but He will fight our battles if we surrender ourselves to Him.

Verse 14. The Lord shall fight for you, and you shall hold your peace. (Just give your troubles to God in prayers and don't try to fight the battle ourselves. The scriptures say the battle is not yours it is the Lord amen.) Now I'm getting close to closing.

Let us go to The Book of Malachi chapter 3 verse 10. And see what instruction what we should do, and God will bless us for being obedient to His words.

Verse 10. Bring ye all the tithes into the storehouse, (Which is the house of prayers) that there may be meat in mine house, and prove me now herewith, saith the Lord of hosts, if I will not open you the windows of heaven, (Now how big are the windows of Heaven? The scriptures teel us that in our father's house there are many mansions. So, that must be some big windows to have many mansions?) and pour you out a blessing, that there shall not be room enough to receive it. So that is letting us know when God open up blessing it is above measures when we apply ourselves to the word of God, be obedient, and be a doer of the word of God. He will meet our needs. What do you need today, my brothers and sisters? God is well able, there is nothing too hard for God that we serve amen.

And the question was at the very beginning I'm about to close now. When we follow God's instructions will he meet our needs? When we follow God's instruction which is his words, he will meet our needs not our greed's. Do not let our greed overcome us. Ask God for the spiritual gifts that when we do it and follow God's instruction His blessings will follow us and overflow us when we are obedient to the word of God. I like when God told Joshua let not this word depart from your mouth Joshua, he said meditate on it day and night and you make thy ways prosper. So, that is why I am telling you about when we be obedient to the word of God the blessings shall overcome us and all our needs shall be met. Not might be, not maybe, but it shall be met. The message God laid upon my heart was, God Will Meet Our Needs! Love you and God love you more. Let us give Jesus' praise amen and bless God.

CHAPTER SEVEN
Love Others As God Love Us

Amen let us give Jesus a hand praise Glory Hallelujah, amen and bless God. First, I would like to thank God for allowing us to be here today on the Sabbath day the holiest day of the week where our Lord and savior commanded us to keep this day holy amen.

Let us go to God in Prayer. Oh, Eternal Father of Abraham, Isaac and Jacob. Abba Father Yahweh Elohim the Great I Am the creator of the heavens and the earth, Jehovah Jireh our provider. Lord God Almighty we thank you for allowing us to be here today on the Sabbath day. Lord, we ask you to decrease us and increase you let it be all of you and none of us. Lord allows us to take self and put yourself to the side for a moment while we bring forth your word to your people. Lord, we ask you to give everyone the ears to hear your word. Lord Almighty we ask that your word penetrates their soul that they might serve you in spirit and truth. Father, we thank you for all that you have been doing and all you are going to do. We give you honor, glory and praise. In Jesus most precious and holy name we pray amen and bless God. Let us give Jesus a hand praise amen.

Now, I always like to ask God for a message for you and I because we all need a word from God. We all came short of the glory of God, and we all need to get back to him amen. And he is so faithful to give us a word. When we come to him bold to his throne of grace.

Before I start, I always like to ask a question and the question is do God want us to love one another? We look at it like all the things that is going on in the world today the trials and the tribulation people killing one another we are wondering do God want us to love one another and the answer is yes. God wants us to love one another, and he laid upon my heart the message for today. Love Others as God Love Us!

49

Jesus told the parable of the Good Samaritan. Jesus said the poor man that was on the side of the road was going to the city and he ended up getting beat and all his belongings got stole stolen and here comes a priest, which a servant of God. He seen this man but went on the other side of the road and walked past by the man that was beaten up. So, then comes a Levi which is another servant of God also seen this man on the side of the road which was half dead, and he also went on the other side of the road and passed up the man. Now here comes the Good Samaritan which did a good deed not just talking about it but doing a good deed. We always tell somebody we love them but show them love. So, the Good Samaritans stopped, and he cared for the man, then he put the man on his Beast and brought him to the end and the servant at the end take care of the man while I am gone and when I come back if I owe you anything extra, I will give it back to you. So, it is all about showing someone that you really love them then just saying you love them. Love is a four-letter word l-o-v-e, but do you really love them? But the beautiful thing is the message said this to let us know what you really mean do you love them or just saying you love them? What is love all about? Love is about a good deed that we show not just saying it amen.

And I like to always ask God for a blessing once again for you and I because we all need a blessing from God. The blessing is May God teach us how to love one another. We must be taught how to love one another. God want us to love each other and love thy neighbor as you love yourself. The word of God tells us to love thy enemies and bless those who curse you and despitefully use you and pray for those who persecute you. That is true love what Jesus the Messiah the savior of the whole entire world in the Hebrew language Yeshua that came down from heaven took on flesh just because he loved us that is action of true love. He came down here and showed us how to live in the word. Not only that, but he also came down here and paid our sinful debt that we could not afford to pay for ourselves. Silver and gold could not pay for our sin. It took the Precious Blood of God, he was crucified, beaten, skin toured apart and did not complain because he knew what his task was to come and redeem us. Then he was nailed to the cross alive my God and he had no sin. He did it all because of the love for us. Then they took him down from the cross and put him in a borrowed tomb. They call it a borrow tomb because he was in there for a little while and he was resurrected. Then he stayed down here on earth and gave some instruction for 40 days to his disciples letting them know what they needed to do for you and I today. Then he went up to his rightful place in the heavens. All this was done because he showed us true love, which is action, the greatest good deed of all times amen. I like to always seal it in Jesus Christ holy name. Alright brother King there you go again in Jesus Christ holy name why in Jesus Christ holy name? So, we will not have any excuses when we see our maker. Because we will meet him one day and you cannot say I did not know, and it will be known that brother Kings told you this over and over like a broken record. So, why in Jesus Christ's Holy Name? Well, I am glad you asked because the gospel writer John chapter 1 verse 1 says in the beginning was the Word and the Word was with God and I love what the Messiah said which is Jesus, Yeshua I am in my father and my father in me, and he said when you have seen me you have seen the father. And the Word was God. Let us pause there for a minute. If the word is God well that means he cannot lie also his words cannot lie. If his words tell you something, you can please believe it is true amen. Because in the Book of Numbers Chapter 23 verse 19 said God is not a man, that he should lie; neither the son of man, that he should repeat: Man will always do like they are God when the word said God is not a man to where he should lie. God cannot lie, man makes promises every day that they cannot keep. One of the things that they tell us is oh don't worry about it I got this; I am going to take care of that do not worry about it. Then suddenly, all hell breaks loose oh well I am sorry, but something came up. Once again God is not a man to where he should lie nor the son of man to where he should repent. I like what verse 20 says God commanded a blessing and he cannot reverse it. The Bible has many promises in it. So, if we be obedient and a door of his word those promises shall come to pass. Because God cannot lie, give him praise Glory Hallelujah! Jesus said anything you ask in my name it Shall be not might be not maybe, but it shall be given unto you by the Father which art in Heaven. Let us give Jesus' praise Glory hallelujah! Now that's enough introduction for today.

Now The Words Today says we are to love one another as God first loved us. God showed his love with action and ultimate good deeds. So, don't tell somebody I love you and don't show action. It is all about showing love, God showed his love not by just saying it but by showing with good deeds and action. You know all this killing one another needs to stop. Show some love and get back to Jesus because that is the only way to eternal life with God. Why we want to go to hell by saying I do not care about you or when somebody do you wrong you want to retaliate. Meaning you want to get back at them instead of giving it to God. Because the battle is not yours it is the Lord, he is the only one who can fix that problem for you amen. So, show some love through Good Deeds and action.

Now let us go the 1st John chapter 4 verse 7 through 12. Remember we said this early that God's word cannot lie so we are going to learn how to follow his instruction.

Verse 7. Beloved, let us love one another: (as the message said love others as God love us) for love is of God; and everyone that loveth is born of God, and knoweth God.

Verse 8, He that loveth not knoweth not God; for God is love. (See God is letting us know though his word what we should do. Now the question always comes up, well I did not know? The thing is we must follow God's words to know what to do not what somebody tell us what to do.)

Verse 9. In this was manifested the love of God toward us, because that God sent his only begotten Son into the world, that we might live through him. (We supposed to be living through Christ Jesus by being obedient to the word of God. The Messiah said I have come not for myself, but I come to do my father's will amen.)

Verse 10. Herein is love, not that we loved God, but that he loves, us, (God love us and his words cannot lie.) and sent his Son to be the prepetition for our sins. (In other words, he came to take care of our sins and paid our debt out in full so we can regain favor with God amen.)

Verse 11. Beloved, if God so loved us, we ought also to love one another. (If God so loved us that he already showed his love that means we should love one another. Well tell me why we hate one another just because you might dress a certain way I don't like, or I don't like the way you do things? That should not cause us not to hate one another.)

Verse 12. No man hath seen God at any time. If we love one another God dwelleth in us, and his love is perfected in us. Let us give God praise! (God dwells in US and his love is perfect in US. That is a mighty God. He wants us to know brothers and sisters to follow his instructions and we shall be blessed amen!)

Let us go to the book of Ephesians chapter 4 verse 32. And be ye kind one to another, (It is time brothers and sisters for us to get back to Christ and quit doing all those devious things to one another. The word is telling us what to do when we do not know what to do my brothers and sisters. Follow his words and meditate on it. I like what God said to Joshua, let not this word depart from your mouth Joshua meditate on it day and night. God is letting us know what to do in a time like now.) tenderhearted, forgiving one another, (We must learn how to forgive.) even as God for Christ's sake hath forgiven you. (God forgave us because of Christ's sake because he came and paid the price for Our sin in full. But now we want to do what we are big enough to do and that is the wrong way amen.)

Let us go to the gospel writer Mark chapter 12 verse 30 and 31. Verse 30. And thou shalt love the Lord thy God with all thy heart, (We cannot con God He knows all things; he is the Alpha and the Omega, the beginning and the ending of our faith. So, we know whether we love him or not if we keep his commandment. The Messiah Jesus said, if you love me keep my Commandments. So, that is letting us know we cannot fool God, he already knows what time it is, meaning he is all knowing. Then he said, love him with all thy heart, soul, mind and with all thy strength. This is the first commandment to love God with everything and surrender yourself to God Amen. And if we do that, watch how things change in our life. We are going to have peace, joy and happiness we are going to understand when things through the blood of Jesus!)

Verse 31. And the second is like, namely this, thou shall love thy neighbor as thyself. (So, if we love ourselves, we should love our neighbor the same way he said,) There is none other commandment greater than these. (Love one another that is what we need to do amen.)

Let us go back to first John chapter 3 this time verse 18. My little children, let us not love in words, (all that is a lot of words that do not have no meaning saying oh I love you so much with no action. Show us some action or show us good deeds. Some people love to say I love you and then they turn around and start talking bad about you behind your back. Show some love. As we said in the beginning God words cannot lie.) neither in tongue; (the old tongue is a bad thing that can cause a nuclear war. So, now when you tell somebody I love you remember to show some action not just words only.) but indeed and in truth. (You can't just say those words I love you and don't mean it? Just leave it alone amen.

Let us go to the gospel writer John chapter 13. Verse 34 and 35. Precept on precept here a little there a little. Verse 34. A new commandment I give unto you, that ye love another; as I have loved you, that ye also love one another. (Nobody loves you more than God. He is telling us what to do, love one another. God is letting us know what time it is brothers and sisters it is time for us to get it together with all the wicked things happening in the world today. The scripture said, in the days of Noah were very wicked and now days are wicked like the days of Noah very Wicked. It is time for us to get closer to God at a time like now.)

Verse 35. By this shall all men know that ye are my disciples, if ye have love one another. (You become a disciple of God if you have loved one another. God has let us know through his word what we need to do at a time like now. The question is, how to get back to God? What must we do to get back to God? Well, simply repent, turn from your Wicked Ways, humble yourself. I like with second Chronicles chapter 7 verse 14 said, If my people who are called by my name would humble themself and pray and seek my face and turn from their Wicked Ways then will I hear from heaven and I will forgive your sin and heal your land. God is letting us know all the answers which is in his words repent and turn back to God start to meditate on his words. Which was in the very beginning amen.)

Let us go to Romans chapter 12 verse 10. Be kindly affectioned one to another with brotherly love; (We supposed to loved one and others as God loves us. We must learn how to love one another, and love is action.) in honor preferring one another.

Now let us talk about our savior Yashua better known as Jesus the Word of God. He showed us how to love by separate himself The Voice the word of God that came down here and took on flesh we heard the story. Then from there he went and paid the price for us by being crucified and then he was hung on a cross nail, my God nailed to the cross then before the Sabbath day they took down and put him in a borrowed tomb. That's how much Jesus respected the Sabbath day amen. He only stay in the tomb for 3 days, then he was resurrected. Before he left, he left some instructions and then how to live. Then he went to his rightful place in heaven, and he did it all because of the love he has for us.

Now we are going to talk about Good Deeds for one another. Let us go to Matthew chapter 25 verse 35. I'm about to get out of your way because I feel in my heart that God has let us know enough today about what we should do. Now the Messiah which is Yashua better known as Jesus going to tell a story about Good Deeds. starting at chapter 25 verse

35. I was a hungered, and ye gave me meat: I was thirsty, and ye gave me drink: (now you heard the story of the Good Samaritan) I was a stranger, and you took me in:

Verse 36. Naked, and ye clothed me: I was sick, and you visited me: I was in prison, and ye came unto me.

Verse 37 Then shall the righteous answer him, saying, Lord, when saw we thee an hungered, and fed thee? or thirsty, and gave thee drink?

Verse 38. When saw we thee a stranger, and took thee in? or naked, and clothed thee?

Verse 39. Or when saw we be sick, or in prison, and came unto thee?

Verse 40. And the King shall answer and say unto them, Verily I say unto you, in as much as ye have done it unto one of the least of these my brethren, ye have done if unto me. (You see a bunch of intellects look at the homeless and say they need to do something for themselves. Well, some of them did, they left where they were living to go somewhere else to make a better life. But just got caught up in a certain situation. The scriptures say the poor will always be amongst us. It is our duty to love and show them the action on what we can do for them. Yes, some of them are on drugs because they got caught up in their problems. But there are many that had no choice because they tried to do better for themselves, and they end up getting caught up with pride and heartaches. That is why we must have Love in our heart, to love one another. Jesus just told the story whatever you do to the least of my brother you have done unto me.

Verse 45. Then shall he answer them, saying Verily (Meaning truly) I say unto you, in as much as ye did it not to one of the least of these, ye did it not to me.

Verse 46. And these shall go away into Everlasting punishment: but the righteous into life eternal. (That is a price to pay my brothers and sisters, whether you know it or not. So, now it is time for us to start getting on track with the Lord doing what he tells us to do through his words. He has told us a lot today about love, now it is the time for us to get it together amen.

The question at the beginning was? Do God want us to love one another? And the answer was: yes, he wants us to love one another as God love us, not just by saying it but by showing good deeds. Yashua better known as Jesus the Word of God showed us love, action and good deed by paying out our sinful debt in full.

As the message said, Love Others as God Love Us! I love you and God love you more. Let us give Jesus a hand praise Amen and bless God.

CHAPTER EIGHT
Seek God

Amen let us give Jesus a hand praise Hallelujah let us give him praise, amen and bless God.

First, I would like to thank God for allowing us to be here today on the Sabbath day the holiest day of the week where God has set aside and commanded that we keep this day holy and serve with him amen.

Now let us go to God in prayers every head bowel every eye closed. Oh, Grace Eternal Father of Abraham, Isaac and Jacob, Abba Father Yahweh Elohim the Great I Am the creator of the heavens and earth. Jehovah Jira is our provider. Father God thank you for all that you have been doing for us and all that you're going to do. Lord, we ask you to order our footsteps because your words say the footsteps of a good man is ordered by the Lord. Order our hearts, minds and lips Lord, allow your people to hear this word that, They will have a hunger and a thirst to serve you in spirit and in truth. Lord You Are God of our life, and we know that you love us because you have shown your Love many times repeatedly. Lord, we ask you to continually lead, guide, direct and keep us in your perfect will in these times of troubles. Lord, we need you because we need to seek after you. And we will make sure that we give you all the honor, glory and praise in Jesus most precious and holy name we pray amen and bless God. Let us give God another hand praise amen and bless God. Hallelujah!

I like to always ask God for a message for you and I because we all need a word from God in these lateral days. There are no big I's or little u in the eyes of God. There are none holy then Jesus. He is the only one that walked this Earth without any sin. Lord, we thank you for everything that you are doing for us. And God is so faithful to give us a message.

Before I get into the message, I like to always ask a question, and the question is; When we seek God will he show us the way through life? The answer is easy; If you have been obedient and being a doer of his word the answer to that question, is he will show us Great and Mighty things. Oh yes, the ones who have been through trials and tribulation and areas of life know that God have shown them many great and mighty things amen.

So, God laid on my heart the message for today is Seek God! Now is the time as we are seeing every time, we turn on the television, social media or your radio we are always hearing tragic things that are going on. Well, that is letting us know what was written in the scriptures from the days of old is coming to pass in our live time. The scriptures said it would be like the days of Noah, the people were very wicked and now is the time many things are going on in the world today. So, God is has given us a warning let us know that it's time to seek him amen.

I always like to ask God for a blessing once again for you and I. The blessing is May God order our footsteps. We need for God to order our footsteps at a time right now. We need to learn how to call out to God I like what Isaiah said, Jesus was going to be our counselor. Well tell me why when things are going bad why we always look at man to fix our problem when man make promises that he cannot keep. But God, will never let us down. Give Jesus a hand praise hallelujah!

I like to seal it in Jesus Christ holy name. All right brother King there you go repeatedly about Jesus Christ holy name. Why in Jesus Christ holy name? Well, I am glad you asked, because in the Book of John chapter 1 verse 1 says in the beginning in the very beginning was the Word and the Word was with God. And I like what the Messiah the Savior of the whole entire world in the Hebrew language Yashua and in the English language Jesus, he said I am in my Father and my Father in me, and when you have seen me, you have seen the Father. Then the scripture said, and the Word was God well let us stop there for a minute. Now we know if the word is God He cannot lie. Then it tells us in the

Book of Numbers Chapter 23 verse 19 says God is not a man to where he should lie, nor the son of man where he should repent. So, as we read the scriptures today let us know that God's words are true and just. His word cannot lie so what his words says when we apply ourselves to the words of God it is going to do exactly what it said it is going to do. Because God's words cannot lie.

Now the Messiah, Yashua better known as Jesus the Word of God said anything we ask in my name it Shall be not might or maybe but shall be given unto you by the Father which are in heaven. Give Jesus a hand praise. That is enough introduction for today.

The Words Today says; To achieve in life, we must learn to seek God through his words and then follow his instruction. If we are not obedient to his words God will not move on our behave. We cannot be just a reader of the word but also a doer of the word Amen.

Now let us go to the prophet Isaiah, the one that prophesied about the Messiah.

Isaiah chapter 55 verse 6 through 11. Seek ye the Lord while he may be what found, call ye upon him while he is near: (Well let us pause for a minute, right there we must realize one thing when we in trouble and things are going bad why we always pick up the telephone and call Humanity? And ask them can you help me out with this situation when we have a mighty God that is the creator of the heavens and the earth that can do. all things. But we still rather go to man and then everything just goes to the left because we trust in man and not trust in the Mighty God that created us.)

Verse 7. Let the wicked forsake his way, and the unrighteous man his thoughts: and let him return unto the Lord, (We see all the trouble that is going on in the world today, now is the time for us to seek God. If we start seeking after God, he can fix all our problems.) and he will have mercy upon him; and to our God, for her will abundantly pardon.

(He is the only one that can pardon us of our sins because Jesus came and paid the price for our sins in full. But now we need to turn from our Wicked Ways my brothers and sisters. It is time for us to get back to God. It let us know that things are getting worser and worser. The time is getting close we don't want what happened in the days of Noah where God destroy Humanity with water or what happen in Sodom and Gomorrah where God destroyed it with brimstone. God is displeased with Humanity, now it is time for us to get back to God he is given us a warning amen.

Verse 8. For my thoughts are not your thoughts, (You see that is our problem we think we are on the same level with God. Remember he is the creator of the heavens and the earth. How can we think that we are on the same level with God?) neither are your ways my ways, saith the Lord.

Verse 9. For as the heavens are higher than earth, so are my ways higher than your ways, (That means we are not even close to God ways.) and my thoughts then your thoughts.

Verse 10. For as the rain cometh down, and the snow from heaven, and returned not Thither, but watered the earth, and maketh it brings forth and bud, that it may give seed to the Sower, and bread to the eater.

Verse 11. So shall my word be that goeth forth out of my mouth: it shall not return unto me void, but it shall accomplish that which I please; (All right now God is letting us know that his word is true and just, and it is going to do exactly what it said it is going to do. His words will not go out and return void. That is a mighty God letting us know that it is time for us to start serving him in spirit and in truth through his grace and mercy. We must learn to be obedient to the word of God and turn from our wicked ways. It is time to stop killing of one another brothers and sisters and get closer to God the one that can fix our problems, nobody else can but him.) and it shall prosper in the things whereto I sent it. (Wherever God's words go it shall prosper amen.)

Let us turn to our older brother David in the Book of Psalms. I would like to call him the praise. He knew how to praise God. David went through a lot of things, he wasn't perfect, but he knew how to praise. God gave him the ability to take down the Giant, God give him the ability to take down lion and bear, God gave them the ability to be a great warrior even though he was not perfect. He did some sinning, but he knew how to cry out to God because he knew that God was the only one can fix his situation. That is letting us know God is the only one who can fix our problems. Anyone who is going through trials and tribulation areas of life God is the only one that can fix it amen.

Let us go to Psalms chapter 63 verse 1 through 8.

Verse 1. O God, (I like the way old David shot out to God.) thou art my God;) David let God know that he can only depend on him. He could not depend on man but can depend on God.) earlier will I seek thee; ("That is what God is letting us know in the message, seek God. That is the only way we can fix something by seeking God.) my soul thirsted for thee; my flesh longed for thee in a dry and thirsty land, where no water is; (Whenever we are in a situation and there is trouble in the land God can fix it.)

Verse 2. To see thy power and thy glory, so as I have seen thee in the sanctuary.

Verse 3. Because thy loving kindness is better than life, my lips shall thee. (That is what we need to do at a time like now is praise God because he is awesome God that hears all prayers that are rendered up into the heaven.)

Verse 4. Thou will I bless thee while I live: (David said he will bless God while he lives and that what we need to do.) I will lift up my hands in thy name.

Verse 5. My soul shall be satisfied as with marrow and fatness; and my mouth shall praise thee with joyful lips: (You see my brothers and sisters it is let us know what we need to do at a time like now. We need to go to God in Prayer and believe in God's words. Because God's words are true and just. We take God's words for granted when we can do all things through him.)

Verse 6. When I remember thee upon my bed and meditate on thee in the night watches. (Meditate on the word of God. I like what God told Joshua meditate on the word day and night.)

Verse 7. Because thou hast been my help, (we should take a page out of David book by letting us know that God will help us when we put our trust in him.) therefore in the shadow of thy wings will I rejoice. (We need to rejoice in the Lord.)

Verse 8. My soul followed hard after thee: thy right hand uphold me. (God is holding us right now brothers and sisters.) Always remember to plead the blood upon our kids, ourselves, our neighborhood, city, parish, state, country and whole world for protection because it is nothing to hard for our God.)

Psalms 53 verse 2. God looked down from heaven upon the children of man, (That let us know God is watching everything that is going on he is an all-knowing God, and he sees all things.) to see if there were any that did understand, that did seek God. (That is the message for today seek God. And that is what we need to do at a time like now. Some might say what must I do at a time like now? The answer is seeking God. I like the story of Lazarus and the rich man when the rich man had told Father Abraham to send Lazarus to dip his finger in some water and put it on the tip of his tongue, I'm paraphrasing a little bit no can do, then he said can you send somebody from the dead to go tell my brothers not do what I did. God have his Servants out there shouting the word to them. It is like today God is allowing his Servants to shout out too many and they are ignoring the word of God. Now is the time to seek God in these troubled times amen.)

Let us go Matthew the gospel writer, we are going to see what our Messiah, Yashua in the Hebrew language and Jesus in the English language have to say.

Matthew chapter 6 verse 33. He is telling us what to do when we say God, we don't know what to do? God said I got my people out there telling you what to do and you don't want to follow my instructions. I have Servants reading my words letting you know what to do at a time like now.

Verse 33. But seek ye first the kingdom of God, and his righteousness; (Not man righteousness but God righteousness, we tend to always follow what man do. If John Doe did this, I'm going to do this also, it doesn't work like that you have to seek God.) and all these things shall be added unto you.

What things do you think he is talking about worldly things? Everybody, I want to be like this person and like that person, I want to have a mansion and a $300 000 car and more money than you can have in a bank. That is not the things he is telling us to seek, it is the spiritual things. All the other things are going to come along with it when you follow his words, be obedient and be a believer in his words. Then he said it shall be added on to you. God is letting us know what to do amen.

Let us go to the weeping prophet Jeremiah chapter 29 verse 11 through 13. Why they call Jeremiah the weeping prophet because he cried out for God's people as we are doing right now, we are crying out to God's people to let them know what we must do at a time like now seek God. That is why Jeremiah cried out he was telling God's people this is the time to seek God.

It is time so Jeremiah 29 verse 11 through 13.

Verse 11. For I Know the thoughts that I think towards you, saith the Lord, thoughts of peace, and not of evil, (Everybody want to be a part of the evil force) an expected end. (God wants to see the best for us if we believe in trust in him.)

Verse 12. Then shall ye call upon me, and ye shall go and pray unto me, and I will hearken unto you. (God hears every prayer that we render up in heaven, but we must be a doer of his words and follow his instruction.)

Verse 13. And ye shall seek me, and find me, (When we seek God, we shall find him.) when ye shall search for me with all your heart. (The scripture says trust in the Lord with all thine heart and lean not to your own understanding, but it always acknowledges Him not humanity but him and he sure direct your path. Give Jesus a hand praise! Amen and bless God.)

Let us go to Jeremiah 33 verse 3. (God is letting us know at a time like now who to call on. You cannot call on anybody else but him. When it just became impossible for man it became possible with God.) This is what the Lord said in Jeremiah 33 and 3.

Call unto me, (He wants us to call onto Him not humanity.) and I will answer thee, (God is letting us know that he will answer us if we call upon him.) and show thee great and mighty things, which thou knowest not. (God will fix all the situations that we do not know about. He will fix it because he is a mighty God, a caring God, and a loving God. He did it because he loves us amen. God want to have a personal relationship with every one of us. How do you get that personal relationship with God? Start praying, believing, trusting his words and turn away from your Wicked Ways. I like what it says in the second Chronicles chapter 7 and verse 14. If my people, which are called by my name, shall humble themselves, and pray, and seek my face, and turn from their wicked ways; then will hear from heaven, and will forgive their sin, and heal their land. We need some healing done now brothers and sisters and to start fixing it we need to seek God.)

As the question was at the very beginning was; When we seek God will he show us the way through life? And the answer to that is yes; God will show us the way he will show us Great and Mighty things. And those who have been through trials and tribulation and areas of life know that God have brought them to it and brought them through it. God is letting us know what to do in a time like now, and that is to seek Him Amen, I love you and God love you more let us give Jesus a hand praise Amen and bless God.)

REVEREND DOCTOR OGDEN L. KING II

CHAPTER NINE
Obedient To God's Words Bring Blessings

I like to thank God for allowing us to be here on the Sabbath day the most holies day of the week and we should keep this day holy amen. Let us go to God in prayers. Oh, eternal Father of heaven and the earth we come to you boldly to your throne of grace making our request known to you because the scriptures said we receive not because we ask not. So, we are asking you to decrease us and increase you let it be all of you and none of us. Give us wisdom, knowledge and understanding of your words so that we can present your words to your people. Lord thank you for everything that you are doing in our life. We give you honor and praise. In Jesus Christ holy name we pray amen and bless God.

I like to always ask God for a message for his people for you and I because God know what we need.

I like to start the introduction off with a question, and question is, must we be obedient to God's Words? And the answer is, if we are obedient to His commandments, the Lord thy God will set thee on high above all nation!

So, the Lord gives me a message for his people. The message that God presented in my heart was Obedient To God's Words Bring Blessings.

In my spirit I thought about the story of Joshua and in the Book of Joshua chapter 1 verse 2 said my servant Moses is dead, now therefore arise, go over this Jordan, thou, and all this people, unto the land which I do give to them, even to the children of Israel. Every place that the sole of your foot shall tread upon, that have I given unto you, as I said unto Moses. He left Joshua some instructions in chapter 1 verse 8 This book of the law shall not depart out of thy mouth; but thou shalt meditate therein day and night, that thou mayest observe to do according to all that is written therein for then thou shalt make thy way prosperous, and then thou shalt have good success.

When we be obedient to God's words it will bring us blessings. That is why God is our everything. No matter what we go through in life God can fix it, because it is nothing too hard for our God amen. God left this testimony for us to live by so that he can do the same thing for us because God do not change. That is the god that we serve.

I always like to ask God for a blessing for you and I. And the blessing is May God lay upon our heart to be obedient to his words. I always like to seal it in Jesus Christ holy name amen. Okay brother King why in Jesus Christ holy name? Well, I am glad you ask, The gospel writer John chapter 1 verse 1 said in the beginning was the Word (Jesus is the word) and the Word was with God and the Word was God (Jesus always was always is and always will be) and the Word was God. So, if Jesus is God the Word that let us know that he cannot lie?

The book of Number 23 verse 19 says God is not a man, that he should lie; neither the son of man, that he should repent: hath he said, and shall he not do it? Or hath he spoken, and shall he not make it good?

That let know that Jesus and his words cannot lie. So, what is written in the holy scripture is true and just. Jesus said anything you ask in my name it shall be given unto you by the Father which are in the heaven amen and bless God.

Now that is enough introduction for this chapter. Let us go to The Words Today, which is; When we are obedient to God's words, Blessing follow!

Let us go to Deuteronomy chapter 28 verse 1 and 2.
Verse 1. And it shall come to pass, if thou shall hearken diligently unto the voice of the Lord thy God, to observe and to do all his commandments which I command thee this day, that the Lord thy God

will set thee on high above all nations of the earth. (When we are obedient to the words of God, he will set us on high above all nation. Remember God cannot lie.)

Verse 2. And all these blessings shall come on thee, and overtake thee, if thou shalt hearken unto the voice of the Lord thy God. (When we follow his instruction.)

Let us turn to Philippians chapter 4 verse 19.

Verse 19. But my God shall supply all your need according to his riches in glory by Christ Jesus. (We need to realize that God will meet all our needs when we are obedient to his words and follow his instructions.)

Let us go to the book of Isaiah the prophet chapter 41 verse 10.

Verse 10. Fear thou not; for I am with thee be not dismayed; for I am thy God; I will strengthen thee; yea, I will help thee; yea, I will uphold thee with the right hand of my righteousness. (We do not have to worry when we have a might God that is the creator of the heaven and the earth if we follow and be obedient to his words that cannot lie.)

Let us go to the Book of Proverbs which I call the book of wisdom chapter 16 verse 7.

Verse 7. When a man's ways please the Lord, he maketh even his enemies to be at peace with him. (God's words will bring many blessings as we continue to do his will as it is written. And he will make your enemies to be at peace with us. For this to work we must apply ourselves to his words doing these trouble times. Do not look at your situation, finances or your circumstances, just keep your eyes upon the Lord amen.)

Who made all this possible for us to live by is our Massiah, the Word of God, Yashua better know as Jesus who came down from heaven and took on flesh to pay out our sinful debt in full by being beat up to where he was unrecognizable. Then they lead him to the cross where they nail him to the cross a live my God and he did not complain. Then they raised him up. Remember he is the Word of God he could have call down a legend of angles bout he did it for us because he Love us. He had mercy for us and said Father for give them because they know not what they do. Then he said it was finished and gave up the ghost. Then they put in a borrowed tomb. Why a borrowed tomb? Because he only stayed there for a short time, three days. Then he was resurrected and stayed on earth for 40 days giving his disciples instruction for you and I today because he is the Alpha and Omega the beginning and the end of our faith. Then he went to his rightful place in heaven. He did all this because he Love us.

What must we do to show God that we Love him and to be obedient to his words that it will bring blessings and God shall become our everything?

Let us go to the Book of the Gospel writer John chapter 14 verse 15 and 23.

Verse 15. If ye love me, keep my commandments. (That is how you show God that you love him when you be obedient by following his commandments then he will become our everything.)

Verse 23. Jesus answered and said unto him, if a man loves me, he will keep my words: and my Father will love him, and we will come unto him, and make our abode with him. (God will become our everything when we are Obedient to his words and follow his instructions)

And the question was Must we be obedient to God's words? And the answer was; If we are obedient to His commandments, the Lord thy God will set thee on high above all nations! When we are obedient to God's words, Blessing follow.

As the Message was; Obedient to God's Words Bring Blessing! Love You and God Love You More!

CHAPTER TEN
The Word Of God Will Defeat The Devil

To start chapter 10, I like to thank God for allowing me to be use for his glory to present his words to his people. I pray that this book be a blessing to the readers soul amen. Always remember to keep the Sabbath day holy because it is the 4th commandment that God assigned to us. And in a time like now with all the things that are going on in the world today. The wars and rumors of wars, the earthquakes, fires, flowed, pandemics, all the troubles going on in the world with people killing people, many sins like the days of Noah. This the time we need the words of God to defeat the devil.

Let us go to God in prayers. Oh, Heavenly Father the Father of Abraham, Isaac and Jacob our Father. We ask you to order our footsteps that we be able to follow your words to be your people. Decrease us and increase you in our life. Allow us to put self the side as we do your will to bring you glory amen.

I would like to start this introduction off with a question; How do we overcome the devil? The answer is, Through the words of God!

I always ask God for a message for his people, and he is so faithful to give a message, and the Message is The Word Of God Will Defeat The devil!

And I always ask God for a blessing for his people, and the Blessing is May God give us the wisdom, knowledge and understanding of His words. In Jesus Christ holy name amen. Why in Jesus Christ holy name? Well, I am glad you ask because the Gospel writer John chapter 1 verse 1 says; In the beginning was the Word and the Word was with God (Which is Jesus who is the living Word, and he said I am in my Father and my Father in me and when you see me you have seen the Father) and the Word was God. If the Word is God that means he cannot lie. Because in the book of Numbers chapter 23 verse 19 says; God is not a man, that he should lie. That means all his words are true and just. And God do not make a mistake. Jesus which is the Word of God said anything you ask in my name it shall be given on to you by the Father which is in heaven. Let us give Jesus' praise amen and bless God. Now that is enough introduction.

The Words Today is How to overcome the devil, is through the words of God!

Mathew chapter 4 verse 4.

Verse 4. But he answered and said, It is written, Man shall not live by bread alone, but by every word that proceeded out of the mouth of God. (That let us know that we need to stand on the words of God to be able to defeat the devil.)

Let us go to Mathew chapter 4 verse 1 through 11.

Verse 1. Then was Jesus led up of the Spirit into the wilderness to be tempted of the devil.

Verse 2. And when he had fasted forty days and forty nights, he was afterward and hungered. (The devil like to catch us at our weakest point when our mind is not on the word of God.)

Verse3. And when the tempter came to him, he said, If thou be the Son of God, command that these stones be made bread. (When we at our weakest point the devil try to test our belief and faith on who we are in Christ Jesus.)

Verse 4. But he answered and said, It is written, Man shalt not live by bread alone, but by every word that proceeded out of the mouth of God. (As God told Joshua; This of the law shall not depart out of thy mouth; but thou shalt meditate therein day and night, that thou mayest observe to do according to all that is written therein: fore then thou shalt make thy way prosperous, and then thou shalt have good success. The word of God is the only thing that can defeat the devil, not even a Nuclear Bomb can stop him.)

Verse 5. Then the devil taketh him up into the holy city and set him on a pinnacle of the temple. (That is when the devil is getting ready to set us up with his tricks.)

Verse 6. And saith unto him, if thou be the Son of God, cast thyself down; for it is written, He shall give his angels charge concerning thee: and in their hands they shall bear thee up, lest at any time thou dash thy foot against a stone. (The devil knows the words of God better than we do because he once dwells in the heaven. So, be careful of his workers, they may know the scriptures as well as you and I.)

Verse 7. Jesus said unto him, it is written again, thou shalt not tempt the Lord thy God. (The devil will always try to make us go against God by making us tempt the Lord thy God. So, do not trust the devil with his trickery.)

Verse 8. Again, the devil taketh him, up into an exceeding high mountain, and showed him all the kingdoms of the world, and the glory of them; (That is the devil's job to paint us a pretty picture of things he does not own. He is the King of lies.)

Verse 9. And saith unto him, all these things will I give thee, if thou will fall down and worship me. (The devil knows we like nice THINGS so he try to use things to make us give up our soul. God gave up his blood to pay out our sinful debt which is more valuable than silver, gold and rubies. That is how much God Love us and the devil knows that.)

Verse 10. Then saith Jesus unto him, get thee hence, Satan: for it is written, Thou shalt worship the Lord thy God, and him only shalt thou serve. (That is where our problems began, we always put other things before our God. Houses, Job, Cars, Family and many other things. When the Word of God which is Jesus said and only him shalt thou serve. God made away out for us through his words and the devil knows that so, do not let him trick us.)

Verse 11. Then the devil leaved him and, behold, angels came and ministered unto him. (Jesus through the words of God showed us how to defeat the devil. The scriptures tell us that the word of God is like a two-edge sword.)

Let us go to Joshua chapter 1 verse 7and 8.

Verse 7. Only be thou strong and very courageous, that thou mayest observe to do according to all the law, which Moses my servant commanded thee: turn not from it to the right hand or to the left, that thou mayest prosper whithersoever thou goes. (We need to follow God's instruction and it will make us strong and courageous to give us the strength to overcome the devil.)

Verse 8. This book of the law shalt not depart out of thy mouth; but thou shalt meditate therein day and night, that thou mayest observe to do according to all that is written therein for then thou shalt make thy way prosperous, and then thou shalt have good success. (The word of God is the key to our good success and give us the strength to stand strong through the troubles of life. Remember the devil do not like us because we are the apple of God's eye. So, it is time for us to get back to God through his words.)

Let us go to Romans chapter 10 verse 17.

Verse 17. So then faith cometh by hearing, and hearing by the word of God. Faith pleases God and when you meditate on the word of God, we please Him. And the word of God will allow us to overcome the devil.)

Let us go to Matthew chapter 18 verse18.

Verse 18. Verily I say unto you, Whatsoever ye shall bind on earth shall be bound in heaven; and whatsoever ye shall loose on earth shall be loosed in heaven. (God is letting us know when we follow his words and instruction, we will have the power to bind the devil and loose blessings into our life. The word of God will defeat the devil!

Let us go to Matthew chapter 5 verse 17 and 18.

Verse 17. Think not that I am come to destroy the law, or the prophets; I am not come to destroy, but to fulfill. (Jesus did not come to change what was written but he came to fulfil and showed us how to follow instruction and live by the word of God.)

Before closing this last chapter, I have to tell you about the one that it possible to make God Our Everything. Yashua better known as Jesus Christ the anointed one of God also known as the Messiah the Savior of the world the Word of God that took on flesh to redeem us from our sins. When came down from heaven he should us how to live on the word of God. Then he went down the pathway to be crucify for our sins he was beat up until he was unrecognizable with his skin torn apart. Then he went to the path to the cross where was nail to the cross a live and he had no sins. Then they raised him up and while he hung on the cross, he did not complain. We as humans complain if we break a fingernail. He could have called a legend of angels to wipe everyone, but he had mercy upon us and said Father forgive them for they know not what they do. Then he said it was finished and gave up the ghost everything that we need and want was bought and paid out in full. Then they took him down and put him in a borrowed tomb. Why put him in a borrowed tomb, Brother King? Because he only stayed there for a short time, three days then he was resurrected. He stayed there on the earth for 40 days leaving instructions with his disciples for us today to live on the word. Then he went to his rightful place in heaven. He did it all for us because he loves us.

John chapter15 verse 13 said; Greater love hath no man than this, that a man lay down his life for his friends.

Hebrews chapter 4 verse 12.

Verse 12. For the word of God is quick, and powerful, and sharper than any two-edged sword, piercing even to the dividing asunder of soul and spirit, and of the joints and marrow, and is a discerner of the thoughts and intents of the heart. (The word of God is very powerful, and the devil knows. That is why he do not want us to meditate on the word of God because with the word we would be able to defeat him.)

Now I am closing; The question is How do we overcome the devil?

And the answer is Through the words of God! And when we become a believer all we must know are these 10 steps.1. God is our strength, 2. God will make away, 3. God is in control, 4. we need God's Grace, 5. God is our Protector, 6. God will meet our needs, 7. Love others as God Love us, 8. Seek God, 9. Obedient to God's words bring Blessings and 10. The word of God will Defeat the devil.

Jeremiah chapter 33 verse 3 said; Call unto me, and I will answer thee, and shew thee great and mighty things, which thou knowest not.

God Is Our Everything!

Love You and God Love You More!

Special Thanks

First: I would like to Thank God all Mighty for using me to Glorify His holy name. By standing on the words of God I have been able to go through all my trials and tribulations of life. When we take care of Gods business, He will take care of our business. God can do all things but fail.

Second: I would like to thank Mr. Charles and Jacqueline Long Manns for preparing me for the past 30 plus years for a time like now.

Third: I would like to thank Apostle Dr. Elbert Bolden for believing in me and putting up with me for 30 plus years. And Minister Refial Papillion for being on the same Team to Glorify God holy name.

Fourth: I would like to thank the Bodies of Christ at Liberty Christian Center for allowing me to teach the Gospel for the past 17 years.

Fifth: I would like to thank Evangelist Pearlie Johnson, Pastor Johnny Offord, Dr. Kip Guilbeau, Miss Audrey Guillory, Wilton J. King Jr., Frances Jones, Louanna Boutte, Pastor Joseph Smith, Brothers, Sisters, Nieces, Nephews and Friends.

Last, But Not Least: My kids Joshua, Jonovan, Latravia, Takeiya, Kiera, Treylon and all my grandkids. And Mrs. Annie Lopez, Mr. Robert and Quippy Quill Team for believing in me. Love You All.

Come
Worship With Us

Liberty Christian Center
1229 West Landry Street
Opelousas, LA 70570
Reverend Doctor Ogden L. King II
ogdenlukeking@gmail.com
revdrolking@gmail.com